BIBLE FACTS ABOUT THE 144,000

By
Bernard Pelton

TEACH Services, Inc.
Brushton, New York

**PRINTED IN
THE UNITED STATES OF AMERICA**

World rights reserved. This book or any portion thereof may not be copied or reproduced in any form or manner whatever, except as provided by law, without the written permission of the publisher, except by a reviewer who may quote brief passages in a review. The author assumes full responsibility for the accuracy of all facts and quotations as cited in this book.

This book was written to provide accurate and authoritative information in regard to the subject matter covered. It is sold with the understanding that the publisher is not engaged in giving legal, accounting, medical or other professional advice. If legal advice or other professional expert assistance is required, the reader should seek a competent professional person.

2009 10 11 12 13 14 · 5 4 3 2 1

Copyright © 2009 TEACH Services, Inc.
ISBN-13: 978-1-57258-557-7
ISBN-10: 1-57258-557-9
Library of Congress Control Number: 2008943158

Published by

TEACH Services, Inc.
www.TEACHServices.com

CONTENTS

Foreword v
Introduction xii
Notes on Matthew 24:36 1
Daniel 12:7-12 7
God's New Testament Timetable 22
Revelation 11 27
The Firstfruits 37
Notes on Matthew 24:45–51 39
John 10:16 and Revelation 18:4 52
Sign of Jonah 63
The Sealing Time 65
Why Exactly 144000 69
The Close of Probation 73
Luke 17:33-37 and Miscellaneous 82
The Kingdom Of Heaven 87
Love 88
The New Heaven and Earth 89
Money Part 1 95
Money Part 2 99
Strong Delusions 104
Miracles of the Bible 107
The Shaking Time 111
So What Do We Do Now? 129
Why God Risked Everything for Us 132
Exaggerating Jesus 136
How God Made the Sabbath 141

List of Abbreviations

1LS	1 Life Sketches
1SM	First Selected Messages
AA	Acts of the Apostles
BC	Seventh-day Adventist Bible Commentary
CWE	Counsels to Writers and Editors
DA	Desire of Ages
EGW	E.G.W. Biography (Vol. 5)
EW	Early Writings
GC	The Great Controversy
LDE	Last Day Events
PK	Prophets and Kings
T	Testimonies for the Church
TM	Testimonies to Ministers and Gospel Workers

FOREWORD

Jesus told His disciples He was to die and to rise again in three days, but it went in one ear and out the other. Why? Because He didn't charge them anything for His advice. If a lawyer had charged them fifty dollars, they would have believed him! But why didn't Jesus know this? He did. He said, "The kingdom of heaven is like unto a merchant man, seeking goodly pearls: who, when he had found one pearl of great price, went and sold all that he had, and bought it." (Matt.13:45-46) And paid for it.

So what's the point? The point is this. I've had to put all this information into a book in order to make you pay for it so that you'd read it. But isn't that kind of mean? Not really. Somebody might charge you a thousand dollars for an ounce of gold, but if they gave it to you for free, you'd think it was fool's gold. Same thing. To get real gold, they'd have to go to Alaska and dig it out of the ground. I've worked at all hours of the day and night for over thirty years digging these things out of the Bible. Then I had to guarantee every word of it or nobody would print it. The information in this book is priceless. Much of it is the words of God that Ellen White "was instructed should be printed in small books, with the necessary explanations, and should be sent all over the world." (TM 117) And like a man who would travel thousands of mile at his own expense, and dig for a year at the risk of not finding any gold at all, I had no idea this would amount to anything.

Jesus created Adam and Eve perfect in a perfect world, and they should have lived forever if they hadn't stolen the forbidden fruit. We are born in a sinful world with an offer of eternal life if we will accept His unlimited love, and give Him our unlimited love in return. He is no fool who gives what he cannot keep (this life) for

v

Bible Facts About the 144,000

that which he cannot lose (eternal life). If we had to pay for our own redemption, it would have opened the door to an endless arguing about how much is fair. Instead, Jesus gave all, and we must give all, which is very fair, especially to us. But if it be given to us for free, we could think of it as fool's gold to be spurned, as above.

According to the parable, "When the king came in to see the guests, he saw there a man which had not on a wedding garment: ...Then said the king to the servants, Bind him hand and foot, and take him away, and cast him into outer darkness: there shall be weeping and gnashing of teeth" (Mat.22:11-13) Whose teeth? In this case, Seventh-day Adventists! How do I know that? Because we are the last generation, and in the judgment hour before He comes. And what is the wedding garment? It is "the righteousness of saints." (see Rev. 19:7-8) It is the robe of light which Adam lost, and that Jesus died to restore before we can enter heaven. All who do not have it will be destroyed "by the brightness of His coming." (2 Thess. 2:8) for not having it for protection against His brightness.

What would you think of a farmer who planted and grew a new crop every year, but never harvested it? He had no interest in mowing and drying it for permanent preservation. He only loved to see things grow, then let it go to ruin and neglect all through the harvest season! What a waste? But if our church only loves to gain new members and never makes herself ready for the marriage of the Lamb, He will come on us like a thief in the night, and He will spew the whole Laodicean church out of His mouth, because we are not ready; fully mature for the harvest. This book can help you be one of the 144000 'very elect.'

In 1844, about fifty thousand people waited expectantly for Jesus to return to earth to take them all to heaven. But He didn't come. They were so disappointed they cried all night! If He had come, not one of them was fit and ready for heaven. They knew nothing about the true

Sabbath. Some smoked and drank, and believed God could burn people forever. They would not have had on the wedding garment (the robe of light) to protect them from the heavenly sights that no flesh and blood can look upon and live. The wicked are all destroyed by the brightness of His coming, because they don't have it for protection. So He would have come on them "as a thief in the night" exactly as He said, and taken away everything they had, even eternal life! This book shows you how to get ready.

But the Millerite Movement was ordained of God, and He continued on with the work He had started. He showed Hiram Edson what had happened in the heavenly sanctuary, then He began to lead the remnant of true believers by miraculous visions and dreams through E.G. White. Many of you know the rest of the story.

When you want a crop, you first plant the seed. Jesus is the Seed. He gave His life (was buried) in order to repopulate the earth with perfect people in His own image, because the first Adam had failed. He couldn't come in 1844 because there was no crop; there were no perfect people to be harvested. For the next century and a half He has been waiting for the crop to grow to maturity and perfection. Perfection means holy hearts, not holy flesh, as will be explained later. The growing season is nearly over, and the harvest time is due very soon. Whether there is much of a crop or not, harvest time can't be put off because "the end shall be at the time appointed" (Dan. 11:27,) and God can certainly keep His appointment. No green or immature produce can be accepted in the harvest. The proof, "And there shall in no wise enter into it anything that defileth." (Rev. 21:27) The Bible says only the "firstfruits" will be harvested first, and the main harvest will happen when He comes, after the plagues. "The sealing time is very short, and will soon be over. Now is the time, while the four angels are holding the four winds, to make our calling and election sure." (EW 58) To "make our calling and election sure" means don't take anything for granted, we need to double check "every word that proceedeth out of the mouth of God." (Matt. 4:4) That's what this book does.

We don't just drift into heaven; we have to watch and be ready. Every Adventist has heard about the future time of persecution, but they may not realize that "persecution" and "harvest" mean about the same thing. War on the saints is "persecution." For example "And the dragon was wroth with the woman, and went to make WAR (persecution) with the remnant of her seed, which keep the commandments of God, and have the testimony of Jesus Christ." (Rev. 12:17) "And it was given unto him (the beast) to make WAR (persecution) with the saints." (Rev. 13:7) If you read further, the beast would "...cause that as many as would not worship the image of the beast should be killed." (annihilated-harvest, vs.15) War is not merely a difference of opinion. War is not war unless somebody gets killed.

But, "Blessed are the dead which die in the Lord from henceforth." (Rev. 14:13) "From henceforth" is a designation of time. It's like saying "from now on." And when is that? Obviously from the first day of the harvest season; the first day of the persecution. And when is that? That's what this book is about, and we are already 164 years closer to it than in 1844! The least doubt about the time will be fatal! Jesus said, "If therefore thou shalt not watch, (don't care enough to watch) I will come on thee as a thief, and thou shalt not know what hour (the exact time) I will come upon thee" (sealing-probation) (Rev. 3:3) This is not His Second Coming which will be very visible, and very noisy. This is not like one of the 27 doctrines to the whole church, or you wouldn't have to worry about missing it. If you are not interested in every detail of end times, you are not watching as you should be, and you lose everything!

The Bible doesn't tell us everything at the same time, or in the same place. We have to dig it out, as for hidden treasure. Prophecy is sealed up by time. It can be revealed only as time progresses, and only as we need it.

Foreword

History is hindsight. Prophecy is foresight. "No prophecy of the scripture is of any private interpretation." (AA 535) Only God can see the future, and "No one is able to explain the Scriptures without the aid of the Holy Spirit." (1SM 411) Thus in God's own time He revealed things to people like William Miller, Ellen White and Joseph Bates; a little at a time, to lead His people safely along, as you will see in this book.

History shows us how God has led us in the past, and how we have suffered by going astray; disregarding prophecy. Right now we are nearing a crisis. "We are standing on the threshold of great and solemn events. Many of the prophecies are about to be fulfilled in quick succession. Every element of power is about to be set to work. Past history will be repeated; old controversies will arouse to new life, and peril will beset God's people on every side. Intensity is taking hold of the human family. It is permeating everything upon the earth....Study Revelation in connection with Daniel, for history will be repeated....We with all our religious advantages, ought to know far more than we do know....As we near the close of this world's history, the prophecies relating to the last days especially demand our study....I have been instructed that the prophecies of Daniel and the Revelation should be printed in small books, with the necessary explanations, and should be sent all over the world. Our own people need to have the light placed before them in clearer lines." (TM 116-117) Thus this book is vital to us, so near the end of time. Ellen White could not write these things because they should not be explained a hundred years ago, and because not one soul of her generation would live to the end.

We need to understand the different Bible meanings of His "coming." Paul's warning "that the day of the Lord so cometh as a thief in the night" certainly doesn't mean His Second Coming, but we must know what it does mean. Most Adventists are clear about His literal and visible coming, but I've never met an Adventist who could correctly explain what it means "to come on thee

ix

Bible Facts About the 144,000

as a thief in the night," yet our very salvation is at stake here! In fact, only the very elect, the 144000 are able to learn "that song" in time to be saved! However anyone is capable of learning it UNLESS they are prejudiced, or negligent, or not watching. Such actions would prove they are careless, and don't really care much anyways. We have to do a lot of home work first to really understand it, and that is why Ellen White was "instructed that the prophecies of Daniel and the Revelation should be printed in small books, (like this one) with the necessary explanations, and should be sent all over the world," and that "Our own people need to have the light placed before them in clearer lines." (TM 117) As you read on you will see how this little book can help you to get ready.

Jesus taught the multitudes for 3 1/2 years, and twelve of them lived with Him day and night. But on the night of His arrest, (at gunpoint, so to speak) they still weren't ready, and they all fled. Yet His twelve, with the aid of the Holy Spirit, became the Christian Church.

Wm. Miller studied the 2300 day prophecy for 12 years, then preached it for 13 years until there were over 50,000 followers. But, they had no idea of Bible perfection (holy hearts), so they weren't ready, and again, only a bitter disappointment. Yet, about 50, with the aid of the Holy Spirit, became a mighty church.

Now there are about 16 million baptized members, and we are nearing the end of the world. This will be the last and only chance to reach Bible perfection in order to be saved. "And there shall in no wise enter into it any thing that defileth, neither whatsoever worketh abomination, or maketh a lie: but they which are written in the Lamb's book of life." (Rev. 21:27) So we have to be ready.

Most everybody knows how to read. Yet "We have only the glimmerings of the rays of the light that is yet to come to us." (I SM 401) That is why Jesus said "If therefore thou shalt not watch, I will come on thee as a thief, and thou shalt not know what hour (the exact time) I will

x

come upon thee." (Rev. 3:3) "Let us strive with all the power that God has given us to be among the 144000." (Review and Herald, March 9, 1905) Why? Because those who aren't that interested are the foolish virgins, lacking oil and not reflecting His image fully. To them He says "I know you not" (Matt. 25:12) These are fatal words, and please don't let it happen to you.

INTRODUCTION

In these studies I have refrained from saying, "in my opinion," or "as I understand it," or "I could be mistaken." My opinion carries no weight at all, unless I restate something already established elsewhere. If by chance I may be mistaken in reading a Scripture, or a dictionary definition, or Strong's concordance, please look them up for yourself. Genuine truth will stand or fall by its own merits. Why should I say "in my opinion" when it's not my opinion, but a reliable definition, an obvious reading, or deduction of facts?

If you are satisfied with your present understanding of last events, and if nothing in the future causes you to question it, then time must be the arbiter. "Work out your own salvation with fear and trembling. For it is God which worketh in you both to WILL and to DO of his good pleasure." (Philippians 2:12-13) But if God's word is misread in the least, or disregarded in the least, God cannot work His will in you to do the right thing at the right time to save you, and you may be lost for your own negligence. God is honored when we cherish "every word that proceedeth out of the mouth of God" (Matt.4:4) "rightly dividing the word of truth." (2 Tim. 2:15)

"Satan tempted the first Adam in Eden, and Adam reasoned with the enemy, thus giving him the advantage. Satan exercised his power of hypnotism over Adam and Eve, and this power he strove to exercise over Christ. But after the word of Scripture was quoted, Satan knew that he had no chance of triumphing." (5BC 1081) Thus the word of God has the power to prevent and to break Satan's hypnotic spell over us if obeyed by faith. Believers are those who believe "every word that proceedeth out of the mouth of God," "rightly dividing the word of truth." Unbelievers are those who doubt God's word, to

Introduction

test some point or suggestion as Eve did. Believers break Satan's hypnotic spell by the proper use of Scripture as Christ did. But unbelievers lack such perfect faith in the Bible. They are willing to accept suggestion in the place of truth. Or they deliberately ignore a part, or a whole Scripture, thus deleting it right out of the Bible, as far as they are concerned. They would correct the Bible instead of their lives; and fail. If any man hear MY VOICE, (instead of Satan's) and open the door, I will come in to him," (Rev 3:20) and this breaks the spell. If we had the power to break the spell ourselves, we would not need the Saviour's example. The willingness to obey lies in us; the power to obey is given with our obedience.

Take for example the Biblical man Naaman, who was not cleansed of his leprosy until he OBEYED perfectly. (2 Kings 5: 13-14) The waters of Jordan didn't part until AFTER the priests actually stepped into the water. (Joshua 3:15-16) Your car won't even start until you obey it perfectly. Even if you owned the company that made it, you have to turn the key like everyone else. Cars are controlled by the laws of nature, which never break. God cannot lie either, and must be obeyed perfectly, as Jesus showed us an example. A friend has the notion that all he has to do is to BELIEVE in the name of Jesus to be saved. He chides me for keeping all the commandments. But I tell him obedience is belief, just as disobedience is unbelief. A very simple deduction.

If you learn anything from these studies, you are merely in a better vantage point to "watch" as Jesus commanded us. We are to perfect our characters, to reflect the image of Jesus fully, and to watch. We have the promise that the Holy Spirit is given to those that obey Him. (Acts 5:32) "These are they which follow the Lamb whithersoever he goeth." (Rev. 14:4) Jesus died that we might become His faithful followers, and we must be just that to be saved.

The Seventh-day Adventist Church has been providentially given the gift of prophecy. Most are well aware of the life and work of E.G. White and the pioneers of our church. Her grandson, Arthur White, was chosen to write a six volume biography of her life from 1827 to 1915. It is a very interesting and thrilling story, and I am reading them for the fifth time. Every Adventist should study these books carefully to understand how God has been and is still leading His church.

Chapter 14 of the fifth volume explains an interesting aspect of prophets in Bible times, with an experience in Ellen White's life to illustrate it. This chapter is titled, "God Reproves His Messenger" and begins with: "Soon after the month-long trip to southern California Ellen White passed through one of the most difficult and excruciating experiences of her life. It involved the developing work in the South, which as has been noted was very close to her heart. It involved her own son, James Edson White. In this experience the Lord in vision severely reproved His messenger.

"Prophets of God were far from automatons. Through many visions their minds were enlightened, sometimes in direct instruction, sometimes through symbols and figures. They were often carried ahead into the future, shown what will take place, and given a line of instruction that would give direction for that situation when the time came. Again, based upon the wealth of the visions given over a period of many years, prophets were often called upon to speak, basing their messages on principles, giving approval to certain proposals and procedures, and pointing out the perils and hazards of other proposals and procedures. This was true with the prophets in Bible times, and it was true in Ellen White's experience.

"She exercised great care in refraining from expressing her own viewpoints in matters relating to the development of the cause of God and in spiritual lines. Often she remained silent when matters were brought before her concerning which she had no foundation in the visions to provide an adequate answer. In a later year when a theological question was placed before her, she remarked, "I have no light on the subject.... Please tell my brethren that I have nothing presented before me regarding the circumstances concerning which they write, and I can set before them only that which has been presented to me."

"On the other hand, many times she was called upon to deal with matters so similar in nature to others that had been clearly revealed to her that she was able to speak promptly and with confidence. Thus at one time she wrote: 'This matter has been brought to my mind in other cases.'"

"It was in keeping with this principle that when the prophet Nathan came before David to build the Lord a house for God, Nathan responded immediately, giving indication that for David to build the Lord a house would be in harmony with God's will. Should not the Lord have a house built for Him? Would not David be the logical man to lead out in this enterprise? But there were factors that at the moment Nathan did not take into account. God called Nathan's attention to this through a vision. It became Nathan's difficult duty to return to David and tell him that the counsel he had given was not right. A house should be built for God, but it should be built by another, one whose hands were not stained with blood." (Ellen G. White: The Early Elmshaven Years, Vol. 5, 188)

Without copying the rest of the chapter, it seems that her son Edson had a habit of over spending and mismanaging money, for which she had counseled him previously. This time, using her own honest judgment, based on their reports to her, she counseled the church officials "to act just as they would act if my son were not there.... I must always stand on the right side of every question. I do not want anyone to feel that I am sustaining Edson in a wrong."

But soon she was told in vision that she "had spoken unadvisedly" and she had to write to them reversing her counsel. Thus God had intervened, which proved to be a real benefit to their work in the South in later years, but embarrassed her very much.

However, the point I wish to make from all this, is not the work in the South, but how God overrules whenever a prophet, working from general principles, makes a mistake that could cause misunderstanding and hardship if not corrected.

"But there are times when common things must be stated, common thoughts must occupy the mind, common letters must be written and information given that has passed from one to another of the workers. Such words, such information, are not given under the special inspiration of the Spirit of God." (1SM 39)

"I find myself frequently placed where I dare give neither assent nor dissent to propositions that are submitted to me, for there is danger that any words I may speak shall be reported as something that the Lord has given me. It is not always safe for me to express my own judgment, for sometimes when someone wishes to carry out his own purpose, he will regard any favorable word I may say as special light from the Lord. I shall be cautious in all my movements." (3SM 60)

With this in mind, let me quote three statements that Ellen White made of her own volition, regarding repeated attempts in time-setting without Bible proof.

"Again and again have I been warned in regard to time-setting. There will never be a message for the people of God that will be based on time. We are not to know the definite time either for the outpouring of the Holy Spirit or for the coming of Christ."(Review and Herald, March 22, 1892)

"We are nearing the great day of God. The signs are fulfilling. And yet we have no message to tell us of the day and hour of Christ's appearing. The Lord has wisely concealed this from us that we may always be in a state of expectancy and preparation for the second appearing

Introduction

of our Lord Jesus Christ in the clouds of heaven." (Last Day Events 33.3)

"God gives no man a message that it will be five years or ten years or twenty years before this earth's history shall close. He would not give any living being an excuse for delaying the preparation for His appearing. He would have no one say, as did the unfaithful servant, "My lord delayeth his coming," for this leads to reckless neglect of the opportunities and privileges given to prepare us for that great day." (LDE 34.2)

Has God made any attempt to correct any of these statements? No. Were any of these statements made by direct vision from God? No. Were any of these statements made under oath? No. They were made solely on her own initiative, based on her own knowledge of God's will to this point. Will they stand the test of time? They have so far. Why do I say that? Let me explain why I say "So far."

For instance, let's say we start out on a long journey with no definite notion of the distance to our destination. Finally we begin to hear convincing proof that we are nearing the end; at mile 1844. But it wasn't so, and most of them were so disappointed and discouraged that they gave up entirely. Some tried to figure out what had gone wrong, then took up their journey more determined than ever. And as they proceeded, several attempts were made to guess at the end. So much confusion resulted from these attempts that we were finally told that we are never to know the definite end of time. The by-word was "SOON." And for over 100 miles (years) all we heard was "SOON."

So where does that leave us? Some of us are still "watching" and wondering. What if Ellen White's statements prove to be wrong? If they are wrong nobody but God Himself has the authority to set the record straight. Nobody knows their map is wrong until they need to use it. If I travel to Los Angeles with the wrong house number, it does no harm until I get to the right street. The exact time to Daniel was sealed up only "until the time of the end" not to the "end of time," so it is still sealed up. But suddenly we discover we had the exact time with us the whole time anyhow! How come? Because the exact time was secured by oath of God to Daniel way back in 534BC, and God is perfectly able to keep His appointment. No harm to the very elect because they are "watching." If they were not watching they could be deceived. But the very elect cannot be deceived and the Holy Spirit can show them these things before it is too late. The very elect are not careless, nor blinded by prejudice. They aren't following the crowd. They follow the Word of God. In the meantime, it served the purpose of putting an end to time-setting. No harm is done unless we fail to follow the Word of God the moment it is called to our attention no matter who says it.

Why haven't we known this all along? Why didn't Ellen White know of this? She did! She said, "Twice Daniel inquired "How long shall it be to the end of time?" (TM 114 bottom line) Since she knew that Daniel was asking Him for the end of time, we can be sure that Christ knew that he was asking Him for the end of time. Especially since He secured it by the most powerful oath in the Bible! BC4 880 says: "No greater oath could be sworn" and proves it from Heb. 6:13, "For when God made promise to Abraham, because He could swear by no greater, He swear by Himself." And this is just what He did in Dan. 12:7. He swore by "Him that liveth forever." The very power of such an oath indicates a corresponding importance of the matter sworn; one of the greatest events in the history of time. He sealed up any understanding of these figures "till the time of the end" not to "the end of time." He could have easily broken the seal by letting Ellen White tell us the truth. Then why didn't He? Because the "time of the end" was still over 100 years away and there was a lot of work to do first. Did He also designate "the time of the end" specifically so we can know for sure the moment we reach it? Certainly He did, or the oath

Introduction

would be pointless, having no definite connection to anything from which to start counting.

In Daniel we learn the exact "time of the end." Here we find the oath that He swore, and the exact "time, times, and a half" (1260 days) of this period, and "when he (beast) shall have scattered the power of the holy people (144000) all these things shall be finished." When "all these things" are finished, means the end of "all these things." What things? The scattering (death) of the holy people (144000) at the end of the 1260 days, which closes probation and triggers the plagues. Christ comes after the 1335 days of the plagues, which we can count because it is 1260 plus 1335, or 2595 days from the day the beast power is given power "over all kindreds, and tongues, and nations" "to make war with the saints, and to overcome them." (Rev. 13:7) "and kill them." (Rev. 11:7) Please don't panic. Every word of this will be explained from Scripture, and made plain as day as you continue to read on. For example, the Bible promises a Saviour at Gen. 3:15, and trusts you to wait for the proof in the New Testament. So I tell you right off, what I know I can prove later. Christ swore to three figures in answer to Daniel's inquiry for the end of time, thus they constitute the periods He calls "the time of the end." The last day of the last figure is the end of time, the day Christ comes. The first day of the 1260 days unseals the time so all we have to do is to count 1260 plus 1335, to the end of time, the day He will come.

Am I not unsealing the date for the end of time by explaining it here? Not at all. Why? Because we can't start counting out the 2595 days until the very first day of the 1260 day period unseals the time to start counting, and nobody knows that yet. How will we know that for sure? Just keep reading for the explanation. If the Bible doesn't remove all doubt of recognizing it, then again, the oath has no power. Read on and you'll see plain as day.

NOTES ON MATTHEW 24:36

"Counsels to Writers and Editors" says: "We should never refuse to examine the Scriptures with those who, we have reason to believe, desire to know what truth is as much as we do. Suppose a brother held a view that was different from yours, and he would come to you, proposing that you sit down with him and make an investigation of the point in the Scriptures; should you rise up, filled with prejudice, and condemn his ideas, while refusing to give him a candid hearing? The only right way would be to sit down as Christians and investigate the position presented, in the light of God's word, which will reveal truth and unmask error ... If the pillars of our faith will not stand the test of investigation, it is time that we knew it." (CWE 44) "We have many lessons to learn, and many, many to unlearn. God and heaven alone are infallible. Those who think that they will never have to give up a cherished view never have an occasion to change an opinion, will be disappointed. As long as we hold to our own ideas and opinions with determined persistency, we cannot have the unity for which Christ prayed." (CWE 37) "There is no excuse for anyone in taking the position that there is no more truth to be revealed, and that all our expositions of Scripture are without an error. The fact that certain doctrines have been held as truth for many years by our people is not a proof that our ideas are infallible. Age will not make error into truth, and truth can afford to be fair. No true doctrine will lose anything by close investigation." (CWE 35)

With these thoughts in mind, we should be willing to take another look at Matt. 24:36. "No man knoweth the day nor the hour" has been taught for many years to mean that no man will ever know the exact time of the Second Coming, or the end of the world. But Jesus Himself said, "If therefore thou shalt not watch, I will come

1

Bible Facts About the 144,000

upon thee as a thief, and thou shalt not know what hour (precisely) I will come upon thee." (Rev. 3:3) This doesn't say we can't know, but only those who don't watch won't know. Disregarding His caution to watch is the same as deleting it right out of the Bible! God can't save you if you would correct the Bible rather than your erroneous thinking. If it be impossible to know the exact time, the Bible is wrong when it says: "Thou must prophesy again." (Rev. 10:11) Every Adventist knows Rev. 10 was fulfilled by the Millerite movement giving the exact time on October 22, 1844. So to "prophesy again" means to give the exact time again, and to do this we must know the exact time as Jesus promises to those who watch.

To not understand the exact time is wicked, or as it says, "and none of the wicked shall understand; but the wise shall understand." (Dan.12:10) Understand what? The exact time given in the very next verses. And when is that? Forty five days later. Look it up.

By READING we are to UNDERSTAND when to flee, he says in Matt. 24:15. And if we understand when to flee, we will also understand the exact time He will come (45 days later) because "Blessed is he that waiteth and cometh to the thousand three hundred and five and thirty days." (Dan.12:12) The "blessing" is translation to heaven; the greatest blessing possible to man. More on this later.

Each of Daniel's four visions reaches to the end of time. Especially the fourth, which ends with Dan 12. Verse 1 says: "and at that time thy people shall be delivered, every one that shall be found written in the book." We speak of being "saved" when we are converted. But we aren't "delivered" until we are taken to heaven. Thus the subject of Daniel 12 is the end of time, not the end of the Dark Ages. "And there shall be a time of trouble such as never was since there was a nation even to that same time." This is clearly the seven last plagues, not the Dark Ages. The plagues are not poured out until after the close of probation, not at the end of the Dark Ages. The Dark Ages ended

2

over 200 years ago, but the plagues still haven't begun to fall. These are obvious errors that must be corrected.

So this leaves us with two problems to solve; what does it mean to "come on thee as a thief?" And does Matt 24:36 really mean that we can never know the time? When Jesus comes there will be only two classes of people on the earth, the righteous and the wicked. To the righteous He restores all that was lost in the Garden of Eden. Certainly He doesn't take anything from them. But from the wicked He takes away everything they have, even life itself, just like a thief. He isn't really a thief in this case because He actually owns us and can do as He wills with His own. Can you steal your own wallet? No. Unless you think it's somebody else's, then you might if you were in the habit of stealing. But this couldn't happen to Jesus. To consider His Coming as merely a surprise and nothing else, is to render the word "thief" meaningless, and ridiculous.

Paul makes the same distinction between the righteous and the wicked at His coming. "For yourselves know perfectly that the day of the Lord cometh as a thief in the night ... then sudden destruction cometh upon them ... and THEY shall not escape. But YE, brethren, are not in darkness that that day should overtake you as a thief." (1 Thess. 5:2-4) Why not? Because the last generation will have the exact time unless they refuse to believe it. (See Rev.3:3) Why would we be told to watch if it be impossible to see anything?

Then what about Matt. 24:36? Regarding this verse we read, "a clear and harmonious explanation of this text was given by those who were looking for the Lord, and the wrong use made of it by their opponents was clearly shown." (GC 371) Thus Ellen White understood the truth of this text and how nonbelievers were making a wrong use of it. "Age will not make error into truth" and if we use it wrong today, we are just as wrong as the scoffers of 1844.

In the book, "The Midnight Cry" you can read the correct explanation from an original Millerite paper dated

Bible Facts About the 144,000

August 22, 1844. You may need a magnifying glass to read it, but it is perfectly legible. Here is that "clear and harmonious explanation of this text" copied verbatim from that paper:

"Concerning the time of that coming, He says in Mark 13:32, 'But of the day and hour knoweth no man, no, not the angels which are in heaven, neither the Son, but the Father.' It is thought by many, that this passage proves that men are never to know the time. But if it proves this, it likewise proves that the Son of God Himself is never to know the time, for the passage declares precisely the same concerning Him that it does concerning angels and men. But can any person believe that our blessed Lord, to whom all power in heaven and earth is given, is, and will remain ignorant of the time until the very moment that He comes to judge the world? If not, then certainly this text can never prove that men may not be made to understand the time. An old English version of the passage reads, 'But that day and hour no man maketh known, neither the angels which are in heaven, neither the Son, but the Father.' This is the correct reading according to several of the ablest critics of the age. The word KNOW is used here in the same sense as it is by Paul in 1 Cor. 2:2. Paul well understood many other things besides Christ and Him crucified, but he determined to MAKE KNOWN nothing else among them. So in the passage first quoted, it is declared that none but the Father maketh known the day and hour, that is, the definite time of the second coming of His Son." (The Midnight Cry, F. D. Nichol, 228)

The object of these studies is to clarify last day events, and make them simple to understand without wresting Scripture. So how does the Father speak to us to make the day known to us? Only by the Bible just like He always does. God sees the end from the beginning. Nothing is hidden from Him no matter how future it is. Everything we need to know is written in prophecy. "No one is able to explain the Scriptures without the aid of the Holy Spirit." (1SM 411) The Holy Spirit is given to those who obey Him. (Acts 5:32) When the time comes for a Scripture to

Notes on Matthew 24:36

be revealed to us, the Holy Spirit moves upon us to believe it for what it says in plain language. A ship may be headed directly toward an iceberg, but it doesn't do any damage until the ship hits it. If the look-out is asleep, or not sure if they see ice or fog, lives may be lost. If we are asleep or confused, the church may be powerless to save us. Even Jesus Himself could not teach the doctors of the law in His day. He had to have common fishermen and tax collectors; those who were not bound by traditional ideas of their own devising. God chose Martin Luther who was a monk, not a Pope, to teach righteousness by faith in Christ, instead of righteousness by indulgences, beads or relics. He chose a sickly uneducated girl of seventeen to establish His last church on earth. By her writings the 144000 will be perfected and enabled to finish His work of righteousness in the earth, providing we read the Testimonies given of God for our safety. You don't have to be young and sickly like she was. You only have to be honest and willing to believe the truth.

There are many things to learn, and many to unlearn, and there is much more light to be revealed. "We have only the glimmerings of the rays of the light that is yet to come to us." (1SM 401) "No one is able to explain the Scriptures without the aid of the Holy Spirit." (ISM 411) All that is necessary to seal up a passage of Scripture is for the Holy Spirit to withhold His aid to understand it, as in sealing up the words in Dan. 12:9, "the words are closed up and sealed til the TIME OF THE END" not to the END OF TIME. This must mean that His hand is to be removed before the end of time, so that the last generation will have the exact time to "prophesy again" as commanded in Rev.10:11.

It should be obvious that when God seals up something no man can break that seal. It is just as obvious that when He reveals it to us, it would be fatal to ignore it. "Surely the Lord God will do nothing, but he revealeth his secret unto his servants the prophets." (Amos 3:7) If God will do nothing without enlightening His prophets first, then He doesn't plan to come as a thief except to the wicked. Those whom He cannot teach by the Bible, are unbelievers by their own choice. Please forgive me for reminding you that a fact is a fact even though a mere piano tuner calls it to your attention. Let's say a man's house is on fire and his five year old son runs to tell him. The fire runs the same course as if the fire chief himself had reported it to him. "The lips of children (the untrained and inexperienced) will be opened to proclaim the mysteries that have been hidden from the minds of men." (TM 116) Let us pray for the Holy Spirit to help us read and understand exactly what the Bible says, no matter who points it out. Everything in the Bible will come to pass just as it is written, whether we believe it or not.

DANIEL 12:7–12

People of no religious persuasion, and people of deep religious conviction both seem to sense that a terrible crisis is about to break upon the world. In all sincerity, Seventh-day Adventists have been expecting the end of the world for many years. Now even the man on the street expects it.

Time is short. "There is need of a much closer study of the word of God; especially should Daniel and the Revelation have attention as never before in the history of our work." (TM 112) These words were written many years ago, but they apply specifically to the short time just before the end, come when it may.

We have had no great revival based on prophecy since 1844. Yet we read: "When we as a people understand what this book (Revelation) means to us, there will be seen among us a great revival." (TM 113) This revival will be great. In fact, it is called the SHAKING, which will separate the wise and the foolish, and close probation for the church! (See Matt. 25:10) The size and strength of the Seventh-day Adventist Church has grown steadily since 1844, but faith and love have waned. We have had no great spiritual awakening based on prophecy since then. On the contrary, we have been rebuked and labeled as Laodiceans by the One who never errs.

"When the books of Daniel and Revelation are better understood, believers will have an entirely different religious experience." (TM 114) Only believers will have this "entirely different experience." "Study Revelation in connection with Daniel, for history will be repeated … We with all our religious advantages, ought to know far more than we do know." Not one word of the Bible ever changes. Then what makes the difference? Time! Time is always changing. Time is the essence of all prophecy. "As

7

Bible Facts About the 144,000

we near the close of this world's history, the prophecies relating to the last days especially demand our study." Why? Because of the time. "A message that will arouse the churches is to be proclaimed ... Our own people need to have the light placed before them in clearer lines." "Advance new principles, and crowd in the clear-cut truth." (TM 116–119) Why? Because a whole century has passed by already.

"Study Revelation in connection with Daniel" means Revelation will help us find light in Daniel. If Ellen White had said, 'Study Revelation in connection with the Testimonies' we would expect to find new prophecy in the Testimonies. The burden of TM 112–119 is that something very vital is yet to be found in Daniel and Revelation. When it is revealed to us, only those who believe it will have the new experience. To those who don't believe it, it is the same as blindness, and can't help them. Some vital ingredient is yet to spark a great work in the last days. What is it?

God has never done anything of real consequence to the wicked without fair warning. He always sends His warnings through the righteous; thus all are warned. "Surely the Lord God will do nothing but he revealeth his secret unto his servants the prophets." (Amos 3:7) God is very specific in this regard, and very consistent. He foretold exactly when the flood would come, 120 years, and Noah believed Him and built the ark. God foretold exactly when Ninevah should be overthrown, 40 days, and they repented; exactly when Christ would come, 69 weeks, and the wise men followed the star. He foretold exactly when the judgment would begin, after 2300 years, and Miller preached it. No warning is possible without the exact time. And no warning is possible to those who don't believe it. This is why He warns them through prophets. Prophets are believers who obey. Why doesn't God reveal prophecy to other churches? "He that turneth away his ear from hearing the law, even his prayer shall be abomination." (Proverbs 28:9) They evidently are not watching, nor listening, so they can't see nor hear. This limits God's aid exclusively to the one and only commandment keeping church. They hear the law.

8

Daniel 12:7–12

"No less a personage than the Son of God appeared to Daniel. This description is similar to that given by John when Christ was revealed to him on the Isle of Patmos. Our Lord now comes ... to teach Daniel what would take place in the latter days. This knowledge was given to Daniel and recorded by inspiration for us upon whom the ends of the world are come." (4BC 1173)

If this knowledge was recorded for us, it must be understood by us. If it was recorded only for those upon whom the ends of the world are come, then all previous generations are excused. And if it is being revealed to us now, then we must be the last generation. However, we have been in error similar to that of 1843.

The error of 1843 like this, "His hand was over and hid a mistake in some of the figures, so that none could see it, until His hand was removed." The editor's note at the bottom of the page says, "But this does not preclude the publication of a chart subsequently which would correct the mistake after the 1843 movement was past, and the calculation as then made had served its purpose." (EW 74)

If the Lord's hand was hiding a human error in the reckoning of the time for the judgment to begin, He may have hidden another error so that we could not perceive the time for the judgment to end and close probation. This seems evident from the total lack of E.G. White comments on Dan. 12:7, 11 and 12 where Christ gave Daniel the exact figures for the ends of the world. (See E.G. White Index 3, p. 83 on Dan. 12:7, 11, and 12.) The truth might have revealed the time. To reveal the time is equal to removing God's hand, which cannot be done until He wants us to know the time. Does this mean that if I give the proper explanation to you now, it would amount to removing God's hand? Not at all. Why? Because you cannot believe anything that I write, even when I quote directly from the Bible itself, except the Holy Spirit opens your mind to believe it. How do I know this? I know it because there is not a single Bible text in this book that has not been in plain sight for

9

Bible Facts About the 144,000

centuries in the Bible, yet until the Holy Spirit is ready for His people to believe exactly what it says, no one will pay any attention at all. Since I began these studies on August 5, 1974, not a single person has believed any of it for any length of time, but has soon given it up. Copying Scripture doesn't add or detract in any way. These words were sealed up in Daniel 12, and copying them to here can not break God's seal. Only God can do that by the Holy Spirit. When time and circumstances are right for the seal to come off, "the wise shall understand" but "none of the wicked shall understand." (Dan. 12:10) Conditions in the church and in the world are all in God's hands, and at His bidding He will open the Scriptures as He did on the road to Emmaus. Not with unpublished words, but with the very same Scriptures we have known all the time. As it was then.

Then why do I work so hard to explain all these things? Because I love to do it. I do this in the wee hours of the night. I often forget to eat because I might lose a train of thought. Did William Miller have any idea his honest and logical Bible studies would be used of God the way they were? Not at all. He nearly panicked at the idea of preaching it. Ellen White had no power to either bring on or to interrupt a single vision. God's work is a labor of love, pure and simple. We do it without even knowing why we do it. He gives us the power to do it, and we just do it. We have no idea how, or when, or what will become of it in the future. We just do it, and keep at it with no thought of what may come of it. Both William Miller and Ellen White were nobody special, but they were moved happily by the hand of God. "For it is God which worketh in you doth to will and to do of his good pleasure. Do all things without murmurings and disputings." (Philippians 2:13–14) Don't argue! Don't complain! I had written little by little, year after year, for over 30 years, and over 100 pages with no thought of a book until I ran across a tiny ad in a magazine. Then I had to adjust the whole work for a book for others to read and not merely for my own pleasure.

All God expects you or I to do, is to obey the rules of common language. For instance, when you read in the

Daniel 12:7–12

Bible and see the word "kill," you know what the word means; the same as everywhere else in the Bible. When you read a passage that applies to you, it doesn't give you the right to disregard it as untrue or impossible. God cannot lie. (Titus 1:2) So if you die in Jesus, you'll be resurrected. Otherwise you need to correct your life and not the Bible. We aren't here to correct (teach) God.

I can give you a copy of this book, but I can't make you read it. And even if you did, only the Holy Spirit can let you understand it without the devil catching it away from you. Why won't an Adventist read it? Or why does he stop after a few pages? If I quote a Scripture out of context, you should call my attention to it. Perhaps it is because I seem to talk about the exact time, which God has sealed up? If so, it is either right or wrong in spite of the seal. I can't break the seal anyway, so don't worry about it. Jesus told His disciples the absolute truth, that He would die and rise again in three days. Wasn't He afraid people would believe Him and prevent His death? Not at all. Why? Because "the words which they needed to remember were banished from their minds; and when the time of trial came, it found them unprepared. The death of Jesus as fully destroyed their hopes as if He had not forewarned them. So (likewise) in the prophecies (of last day events) the future is opened before us (today) as plainly as it was opened to the disciples by the words of Christ. The events connected with the close of probation and the work of preparation for the time of trouble, are CLEARLY PRESENTED. But multitudes (of Adventists) have no more understanding of these IMPORTANT TRUTHS than if they had never been revealed. Satan watches to catch away every impression that would make them (us) wise unto salvation, and the time of trouble will find them (us) unready." (GC 594)

But Ellen White goes on, "When God sends to men warnings so important that they are represented as proclaimed by angels flying in the midst of heaven, He requires every person endowed with reasoning powers to heed the message. The fearful judgments denounced against the worship of the beast and his image (Rev. 14: 9–11) should lead all (every Adventist) to a diligent study of the prophecies to learn what the mark of the beast is, and how they are to avoid receiving it. But the masses of the people (SDA's) turn away their ears from hearing the truth and are turned unto FABLES." What fables? These fables. (1) That the 144000 is a symbolic number. But John only wrote the number God told him to write and he didn't have to guess at it. Thus to doubt the number is to disbelieve God, and accuse Him of error. But God cannot lie. See Titus I:2. (2) That no man can ever know the day and hour. But Jesus Himself said only those who do not watch (when they should be watching) won't know the exact time. (3) That there is no more light to be revealed. Not so. "We have only the glimmerings of the rays of the light that is yet to come to us." (1SM 401) and you are reading some of that light right now. (4) That the 144000 are translated "without seeing death." Ellen White never said this anywhere. "Behold, the Lord cometh with ten thousands of his saints." (Jude 14) Saints are people, not angels. If you think Jude meant angels, why would he say ten thousands? Angels are an innumerable number; many millions at least! (See Dan. 7:10) And people could not come with Him unless they had gone to heaven before He comes. That is why the 144000 are called the "firstfruits" of the harvest. (5) That all three figures given under oath in Dan. 12 apply to the Dark Ages. This has already been proven wrong. All these things will be explained in more detail as you read on, and they must be correctly understood or He will come on us as a thief instead of the Saviour.

God has always used the most unlikely persons to do His bidding. "The lips of children (the untrained and inexperienced) will be opened to proclaim the mysteries that have been hidden from the minds of men." (TM 116) "God hath chosen the foolish things of the world to confound the wise; and God hath chosen the weak things of the world to confound the things that are mighty; and base things of the world, and things which are despised,

Daniel 12:7–12

hath God chosen, yea, and things which are not, to bring to nought things that are: that no flesh should glory in his presence." (I Cor. I: 27–29) "And for this cause God shall send them strong delusion, (on purpose) that they should believe a lie." (2 Thess. 2:11) Who is 'them'? Anyone who prefers to be prejudiced, or too careless to believe the truth. Perhaps those who see only me, and not God, in the words they read in this book. In Matt. 27:63 prejudice turned Jesus into "that deceiver!" "Prove all things; hold fast that which is good." (1 Thess. 5:21)

Sad to say, there is another reason why Adventists are "turned off" from reading or believing last day events? For instance, do you know of a single Adventist who is so in earnest about perfecting his/her character "to reflect the image of Jesus fully" that they "prize victory and salvation enough to perseveringly plead and agonize for it?" (See "Early Writings" 269–273) Yet Ellen White said: "Let us strive with all the power that God has given us to be among the 144000." (Review and Herald, March 9, 1905) Why? Because they are the only Adventists (of the last generation) that will be sealed and saved. Only the great multitude of Rev.7:9 will greet Him when He comes. Their names are never entered on the church records. The great multitudes are saved out of the worldly churches, not the Adventist church; "not of this fold." This will be proven clearly to anyone who will believe the Bible as it reads. Besides, why would she tell us we have to strive with all our power if there is an easier way? Part of striving for the victory is to know for sure how, when, and where to be ready so He won't come on us as a thief and take away all hope of salvation for not knowing what we are supposed to do. If you love truth, read on. If not, you automatically love error, and are deceived already for not knowing the truth, nor wanting to. After all, if I wrest Scripture you can't correct me if you don't know better Scriptures to use instead. And if heaven is a real place, then the way to it is just as real, and mustn't be mistaken.

The Bible tolerates no haphazard interpretations, no elements of unbelief, no preconceived notions, nor traditional interpretations. We cannot take anything for granted. A strict application of the words of Christ to Daniel will reveal the exact time for the judgment to end.

"And I heard the man clothed in linen which was upon the waters of the river, when he held up his right hand and his left hand unto heaven and sware by him that liveth forever that it shall be for a time, and times, and an half; and when he shall have accomplished to scatter the power of the holy people, all these things shall be finished." (Dan.12:7)

"A time, and times, and an half" is 1260 days. Uriah Smith applied these days, as years, to the papal supremacy of the Dark Ages. (See his notes on Dan. 12:7.) Our 4BC 880 does the same. It has become standard Adventist teaching. But Daniel had asked, and Christ had given these figures in answer to his inquiry for the END OF TIME. (TM 114 bottom line) The vision had already reached to "the time thy people shall be delivered" at Dan. 12:1, prompting Daniel to inquire for the exact end of time, which they then discussed for the rest of the chapter.

What does the word "delivered" mean? When I get mail from UPS it is delivered to my door. It may have been "saved" from fire or flood, but that doesn't deliver it to my door. Likewise, the saints may think they are saved, but they are not "delivered" until they are translated to heaven. Every one of Daniel's four visions reaches to the end of time. Neither is there the slightest word or precedent anywhere in the Bible for these figures to revert back to any former time or event in an honest understanding of the 1260 days, or years.

Applying the 1260 days, AS YEARS, to the Dark Ages, for all practical purposes renders them null and void of meaning for us, because they are long past, and therefore of no consequence to us. Neither do we pay the slightest attention to the oath given to secure them. But to give them a second application as 1260 DAYS (3 1/2 years)

Daniel 12:7–12

ending with the World Sunday Law, makes them of the most vital importance to us. It closes probation forever!

To discover clear Bible proof of this fact, backed by the greatest possible oath of Christ, could indeed spark a new revival and an entirely different religious experience. The angel Gabriel was sent to explain the various time elements of the 2300 day prophecy, including the exact time of Christ's baptism as the Messiah. But no oath was sworn to secure that date. Yet Christ Himself appeared to Daniel, and swore the most solemn oath in the Bible to secure the exact time of His Second Coming! But our standard church teachings completely ignore His oath, and apply these dates to the Dark Ages; wresting Scripture in the process!

The Bible deals in three kinds of time, prophetic time, probationary time, and historic time. Prophetic time (day for a year) applies only to the end of the 2300 year prophecy. Probationary time applies only to the end of probation, after which the plagues are poured out immediately. Historic time applies only until the end of human history, the return of Jesus. Actually Daniel asked "How long?" three times if we include Daniel 8:13. The answer in the next verse gives us the end of prophetic time in 1844. The other two in Daniel 12:7 and 12 give us the end of probationary time and the end of world history, the return of Jesus. This is why the Bible speaks of the ends (plural) of the world. The world doesn't end three times; only the ends of three kinds of time.

As a result of the 1260 days of Daniel 12:7 Jesus said, "All these things shall be finished." But what can we say was finished if we apply these days to the Dark Ages? Certainly not the beast power, for its wounded head is still yet to be healed. Nor any of the three kinds of time. Prophetic time would not end until 1844 at the end of the 2300 years, 46 years after 1798. Probationary time and historic time may be short, but neither has ended yet. So nothing prophetic was finished in 1798, showing that He could not have sworn His figures to mean the years of the

15

Bible Facts About the 144,000

Dark Ages, unless to make us think so for a while until it served some other purpose.

Nowhere in the Bible are these days ever written as years, only as days, months, or times. Changing them into years was expedient only during prophetic time. "Prophetic time closed in 1844." (EW 243) The method of calculation, using a day for a year, ended with it. For instance, a carpenter uses his steel tape to the edge of a roof. To go beyond that into open space his method of calculation must change to miles, or light years!

But this could not prevent God from having another time prophecy based on literal time, for He had already commissioned the church to "prophesy again." To do this, we must have another time prophecy, and it must be straight from the Bible. If it should lack a "Thus saith the Lord," we have nothing. But we do have such a prophecy, and backed by the greatest possible oath of Christ Himself. All last day events are in literal time. Days should not be changed into years after 1844 under any circumstances.

"Study Revelation in connection with Daniel, for history will be repeated." (TM 116) If history is to be repeated, then the prophecies corresponding to those histories will be repeated as well. This makes the standard prophecies of Revelation dual prophecies. The first application of a dual prophecy serves only to teach. It proves the accuracy and reliability of the prophecy, giving us skill and confidence to prophesy again for its second application. It matches history with prophecy while both are past, thereby teaching us to match history with prophecy again while both are yet future. This is exactly how it was with the 2300 day prophecy. The earlier dates matched history perfectly by the day for a year rule. This made it possible to set the 1844 date before it happened. This is why prophecy is so dependable. "We have a more sure word of prophecy; whereunto ye do well that ye take heed." (2 Peter 1:19)

Daniel 12:7–12

The end of the 1260 days, spoken of in Dan. 12:7, marks the beginning of the 1335 days of Dan. 12:11–12. They connect together here. Thus the events which mark the end of the 1260 days are explained as marking the beginning of the 1335 days. The end of the investigative phase of the judgment triggers the executive phase of the judgment. The end of probation is the beginning of the plagues.

"And from the time that the daily sacrifice shall be taken away, and the abomination that maketh desolate set up, there shall be a thousand two hundred and ninety days. Blessed is he that waiteth, and cometh to the thousand three hundred and five and thirty days." (Dan. 12:11–12)

Segments of time such as these are useless until demonstrated to fit between points undeniably established by the Bible. Can this be done with the 1335 days given here? It certainly can. We already know the end of it to be the return of Christ, for it is the last figure given to Daniel's last inquiry for the end of time. The beginning of it is marked off by two events; thus they trigger it. These two events are unmistakably identified: (1) ("the daily sacrifice shall be taken away") No more intercessory work between God and man closes probation. (2) ("the abomination that maketh desolate set up") The World Sunday Law causes every soul on earth to worship the beast, taking the mark, or to worship God on Sabbath to be sealed (killed.) Probation closes when the saints are all sealed, by their death. Everyone's destiny is sealed when they die.

Both events happen simultaneously in this way. The very day the World Sunday Law takes effect, the destiny of every person on earth will be decided by each individual's own choice. Those who love truth will obey the everlasting gospel as preached by the three angels of Rev. 14. On pain of death by the beast, they still trust in Jesus in spite of all that man threatens to do to them. Confessing Jesus as their Saviour, their sins are blotted out and they receive the seal of God; death. "And they overcame him by the blood of the Lamb ... they loved not their lives unto the death." (Rev.

17

12:11) They have "the faith of Jesus." The faith of Jesus is the faith to die rather than to sin.

But those who love not the truth will believe a lie and "drink of the wine of the wrath of her fornication." (Rev. 14:8) In spite of all that God promises to do FOR them, or to do TO them, they refuse to believe Him; they take the mark of the beast. "And all ... shall worship him (the beast) whose names are NOT written in the book of life of the Lamb." (Rev.13:8) They follow Satan, not the Lamb of God. The true church is the Lamb's wife; (see Rev. 19:7–8) Satan's church is the great whore, the mother of harlots. (See Rev. 17:1–7) To flirt with Satan is spiritual adultery.

Thus, "In the issue of the great contest, two parties are developed." (7BC 980) But neither group will ever petition Christ again for forgiveness after that day. Those who are forgiven need no further forgiveness for they are sealed and will never sin again. Those who worship the beast grieve away the Holy Spirit, without which repentance is impossible (the unpardonable sin) and their names are blotted out of the book of life. The World Sunday Law is the deciding factor. It serves to block all further redemption and desolates the earth. It is the "abomination that maketh desolate." For the lack of petitioners the intercessory work of Jesus ceases. The end of probation is the beginning of the 1335 days of terrible trouble and plagues. "The substitution of ... Sunday in the place of the Bible Sabbath is the last act in the drama." (7T 141)

Only one division of time now remains in question: the 45 days from 1290 to 1335 days. A very special blessing is promised to those who wait through these last 45 days. What is it? No blessing could come to the wicked during these 1335 days of the plagues, because probation closed before they began to be poured out. So this 45 days pertains to the righteous who receive the greatest possible blessing, translation to heaven with Jesus at the 1335th day if they wait these last 45 days or the time of Jacob's trouble.

Daniel 12:7–12

What are the circumstances of the righteous during these 45 days of waiting? "I saw the saints leaving the cities and villages, and associating together in companies and living in the most solitary places. Angels provided them food and water, while the wicked were suffering from hunger and thirst. Then I saw the leading men of the earth consulting together, and Satan and his angels busy around them. I saw a writing, copies of which were scattered in different parts of the land, giving orders that unless the saints should yield their peculiar faith, give up the Sabbath, and observe the first day of the week; the PEOPLE (not papal police) were at liberty after a certain time to put them to death." (EW 282-283) If they can find them; dogs can pick up a scent only by the power of God. Electronic surveillance and human eyes and ears likewise!

This shows the relation of the death decree to their flight to the wilderness. Evidently they will agree upon a definite time to flee, for it is a general exodus of the saints to the woods. We can assume the exodus to be global, since the decree will be global. Ellen White gives no exact time to flee, for she was not given exact times for any last day events. But it is not left to chance because God Himself makes known the day and the hour as already explained. In fact He made it known to Daniel in the figures and words that were sealed up until "the time of the end." To reveal the time, all He need do is to remove His hand and open our minds to read correctly what we see in the Bible, and believe it.

Only the last generation, the living, will need to know when to flee, for those who will not live to then need not know the time. Jesus Himself directs you to the words that were sealed up and cautions you to understand. "When ye therefore shall see the abomination of desolation, (Sunday law) spoken of by Daniel the prophet, stand in the holy place, (standing in the fourth place of the ten commandments or the holy place) (whoso READETH, let him UNDERSTAND) then let them ... flee into the mountains." (Matt. 24:15) So we get the exact time to flee, from the Bible He says; by READING. A marginal reference from this verse (Matt. 24:15) will take you to Dan.12:11 and the 1290th day on which to flee and wait for the 1335th day of the next verse. No other signal can be expected, for this is the only one given. It serves no other purpose. God communicates by the Bible, and the days can be counted with absolute certainty; "the more sure word of prophecy." Those who don't believe the Bible, but wait for an audible voice will hear only Satan's impersonation instead. The Bible is God's word, and "every word that proceedeth out of the mouth of God" is not audible, but is sufficient for believers.

"A decree went forth to slay the saints, which caused them to cry day and night for deliverance. This was the time of Jacob's trouble." (EW 37) "And at that time thy people shall be delivered, every one that shall be found written in the book." (Dan.12; 1) Both of these statements apply to the same event at the end of time, the last 45 days between 1290 and 1335 days, are secured by His most powerful oath in Dan.12;7. He swore to only three dates; 1260 days from the day the beast receives power, to the close of probation; 1290 days from the close of probation to the flight to the wilderness; and 1335 days from the close of probation to the return of Jesus.

"But pray ye that your flight be not in the winter." (Mat. 24:20) This practically pinpoints the day of the year if we remember three facts. (1) We know the death decree will be global. (2) Summer and winter alternate north and south of the equator, leaving only three months of spring and fall when winter could be avoided over the whole earth at one time. And (3) It takes at least 45 days beyond winter to warm the ground enough to produce the earliest shoots to eat, March 21 to May 5, for instance. We know Jesus considered this, because He said, "And except those days (the only days other than winter) should be shortened, there should be no flesh saved." (Matt. 24:22)

"Flesh means our bodies. He says we couldn't survive the elements if we fled before May 5th, for example.

Daniel 12:7–12

This would leave only the 45 days from the 1290th to the 1335th day, or it would force the opposite hemisphere into winter. Thus He should return the last day of spring, or the last day of fall. Depending which hemisphere you are in at the time, the next day would be the first day of winter.

"But go thy way till the end be; for thou shalt rest, and stand in thy lot at the end of the days." (Dan.12:13) This verse is self explanatory if we keep it strictly in context of the discussion of time in Dan 12. Daniel was to rest (die) and stand (be resurrected) in his lot (one of the two resurrections) at the end of THE days. "The" is definite and limits us to the days they were discussing, not just any random days. Daniel must wait in the grave for the resurrection "at the end of THE 1335 days" under discussion.

GOD'S NEW TESTAMENT TIMETABLE

Standard Adventist doctrine teaches that the 1260 days and the 1290 days of Daniel 12:7 and 11 ended simultaneously in 1798. Since 1335 is 45 days longer, it came to 1843. This would be roughly at the first disappointment, which was a mistake, and nothing happened! It renders the most powerful oath in the Bible absolutely pointless, as if God had made a mistake! But God doesn't make mistakes. We make mistakes. God could have easily said 1336 days, if He had really intended to cover that period of time. But He didn't. The 1335 days begin the very day probation closes, triggering the plagues, and ends the very day of Jesus' Second Coming. Both ends are exact, and end on two of the most significant days of human history; the close of probation, and the return of Christ!

Time is funny stuff. It runs so smoothly and so transparently that it cannot be measured by itself. Only by counting the dependable cycles of nature can we tell time at all. Jesus set up our days and years by the rotation of the earth on its axis, and its orbit around the sun. These are tamper proof segments of time upon which all other time is in fractions (seconds, minutes, hours) or in multiples (weeks, months, years.)

Jesus also sets up kingdoms, "that the living may know that the Most High ruleth in the kingdoms of men, and giveth it to whomsoever he will, and setteth up the basest of men." (Dan. 4:17) Since He has the power to set up "the basest of men" (by wars), how can we doubt that He can also do it to fit precisely His days and years of prophecy? He doesn't miss by one year, as in 1843. Neither is it pure coincidence that the papacy reigned 1260 years and will return again for exactly 1260 days.

God has already appointed the end of time. "For yet the end shall be at the time appointed." (Dan. 11:27 and

35; Acts 17:31) If a nurse should say to you, "You have an appointment with the doctor, but I can't give you the time," you would have no appointment because the time itself is the appointment. An "intention" has no substance, and is not reality. Thus when the Bible says, "the end shall be at the time appointed" it means God has given us the exact time, and He will never have to change it, because He is able to keep His appointment. God cannot lie, so this is reality, not fiction.

If you should die suddenly, the appointment is automatically taken care of. At death your destiny is to be determined in the judgment, based on your record of faith, or lack of faith in Jesus to overcome sin in your life. All the dead are raised in one or the other of the two resurrections, both of which are safely beyond the reach of Satan to molest. But the living he can still tempt, and try to deceive them to disregard the Bible arrangements as to when to flee, and to be ready to meet Christ on His terms, not ours. If we aren't there, for not following exactly what is clearly written in the Bible, it is because we weren't watching as He commanded. To be certain the 1260 days (years) of the Dark Ages are not confused with the 1260 days of the beast power still future, they are infallibly written into the New Testament timetable symbolized by the seven trumpets of Revelation chapters 8 through 11.

It is common knowledge that a trumpet call is a call to war in Bible prophecy (see Uriah Smith or the SDA Commentaries). Wars are so well known and documented that their dates are never in dispute. But Uriah Smith had never seen a motor truck, a tank, an airplane, or an atom bomb. So he adapted everything to the 19th century, and it has been standard Adventist doctrine ever since. But now we must update our timetable to "present truth" or commit a fatal error for our neglect of diligent Bible study.

We need to consider the last three trumpets to pick up the sequence again. Each of the last three trumpets were to signal unprecedented woe on the whole earth (world wars). "Woe, woe, woe, to the inhabiters of the earth by reason of the other voices of the trumpets of the three angels, which are yet to sound!"(Rev. 8:13)

These three "woes," then must correspond to the 5th, 6th, and 7th trumpets which are World Wars I, II, and III. Probation closes at the seventh trumpet which is clearly indicated by Rev. 11:15–18. "And the seventh angel sounded; and there were great voices in heaven, saying, The kingdoms of this world are become the kingdoms of our Lord, and of his Christ; and he shall reign for ever and ever ... and shouldest destroy them which destroy the earth."

Each trumpet commences a new war, thus the previous one would also include its aftermath. The fifth began at World War I and includes the Great Depression which followed it. The sixth begins World War II and continues to the close of probation, or until the seventh signals the plagues and the War of Armageddon. Please remember that the plagues follow immediately at the close of probation, during which Satan has full control of the wicked, and the world is in total anarchy! "The same shall drink of the wine of the wrath of God, which is poured out without mixture" (no mercy). (Rev. 14:10) God simply lets the wicked follow Satan's ideas of total freedom from restraint. Total selfishness. Every man for himself. Do it unto others, before they do it unto you, is just the opposite of "Do unto others as ye would that they do unto you." (Luke 6:31) But Satan cannot touch the righteous, except to threaten them and test their faith in Jesus.

At this point we backtrack to pick up God's providence as He warns the world and saves His own. Rev. 10 was fulfilled by the Millerites, warning the world that "there should be time no longer." (Rev. 10:6) This meant "prophetic time" that ended October 22, 1844. The end of the 2300 year prophecy of Dan. 8:14 resulted in the establishment of the Seventh-day Adventist Church to raise up a people in the image of God to "keep the commandments of God and have the faith of Jesus," as a witness to the world.

"Thou must prophesy again" The word AGAIN means "to do it once more; to repeat it." To do something different, would not be an AGAIN, but we must do the very same thing again. And what is that? The Millerites preached the exact day for Jesus to come, and they did it with an exact calculation of Bible prophecy. Their math was perfect to the very day. And this we must repeat again. Revelation 11 is the experience of the 144000 as they bring the world to follow God's Law, and not man's law, (Sabbath or Sunday) then probation closes at verse 15. This places Rev.11 where it belongs in God's New Testament timetable. Not in the French Revolution, but at the close of probation.

Since "Great Controversy" chapter 15 explains Rev. 11 as the war on the Bible during the French Revolution, and since this Scripture clearly brings us right up to the close of probation at the seventh trumpet, how can we resolve the problem without wresting Scripture, or discounting the pen of inspiration?

"Study Revelation in connection with Daniel, for history will be repeated." (TM 116) If history is to be repeated, then both prophecy and history must be repeated again, and "Thou must prophesy again." To do something different, or to try to avoid it, is impossible because the word "MUST" makes it absolutely imperative, unavoidable, and mandatory. We know this from the experience of Jonah who tried to side-step the Lord's command to prophesy.

"The world-wide dissemination of the same teachings that led to the French Revolution--all are tending to involve the WHOLE WORLD in a struggle similar to that which convulsed France." (Ed.228) What happened in France (complete anarchy) will be repeated worldwide in the plagues. Thus the dual prophecy above. The French Revolution was a war on the WORD of God, and people were slaughtered unmercifully. But Satan failed and the Bible prevailed to give the world the greatest freedom ever known. He tries again with a war on the Law of God, (Sunday verses Sabbath) and God's people are killed at Rev. 11:7, resurrected at verse 11, ascend up to heaven at verse 12, and the seventh trumpet closes probation at verse 15. Thus history is repeated. The same prophecy covers both events as a dual prophecy. Now let's study Rev.11 in detail.

REVELATION 11

(1) "And there was given me a reed like unto a rod; and the angel stood, saying, Rise, and measure the temple of God, and the altar, and them that worship therein." In Rev. 11, as in Rev. 10, John prefigures the church. What happens to John in a sense happens to the church; a definite parallel. When John was given a little book to eat, it was sweet in his mouth, but bitter in his stomach. Likewise, the church was first delighted and later disappointed as they digested the book of Daniel in 1844.

"Now John is told to "Rise." This is a direct order for him (the church) to rise up. But what church? The same church that ate up the little book with such disappointment, and is so sick at heart, and feeling so miserable about it. "And measure the temple of God." What with? Obviously the "reed like unto a rod." Something is given to the church for the purpose of measuring. What is it? In Strong's Concordance, the word "reed" is from the Greek "kalamos" and defined as "a reed (its plant or stem) by implication, a pen, reed." In those days, "pen" and "reed" were practically synonymous. In III John 13, pen and ink are used together, yet the word "pen" was translated from the same "kalamos." Guided by the context, when they saw "kalamos" with ink they called it a pen, but when they saw it "like unto a rod" they called it a reed. In a minute we'll try it as a pen, rather than a reed, which the translators could have honestly done.

But first let's look up "rod" in Strong's and find it is from "rhabdos," meaning "a stick or wand (as a cudgel, a cane, or a baton of royalty) rod, scepter, staff." Several texts in Revelation speak of a "rod of iron" and clearly indicate the reign of Christ; and in every case the "rod" is from "rhabdos." So if the reed (or pen) is not a rod, but only "like unto a rod" and if that rod (from rhabdos) indicates divine

Bible Facts About the 144,000

authority, then this verse could have said, "And there was given me a pen like unto divine authority," or as Adventists would say, "the pen of inspiration." E.G.White was given her first vision only two months after the disappointment of 1844. Her visions were miraculous works of God to establish the Seventh-day Adventist Church, to measure and to fit a people for heaven, and to preach the three angels' messages before His return.

Although the people were willing to meet Jesus in 1844, they weren't ready. They knew nothing of the true Sabbath, correct baptism, or the sanctuary service. Some danced, smoked, and used tea, coffee, and alcohol. They believed in an ever burning hell, and the immortality of the soul. Through visions and dreams of Ellen White, God corrected all this and more. She wrote "Testimonies for the Church" to measure and to correct "them that worship therein." When the 144000 are thus corrected in every respect and "are without fault before the throne of God," the scene will advance immediately to the last act in the drama, and to its desired conclusion.

(2) "But the court which is without the temple leave out, and measure it not; for it is given unto the Gentiles: and the holy city shall they tread underfoot forty and two months." We are not to use the "Testimonies" on non-Adventists. They are to be used only to correct and instruct those who willingly come to Christ for help. "As many as I love, I rebuke and chasten--be zealous therefore, and repent" He says to His church, but He never forces anyone. Even His chastening, correcting life and doctrines, must be accepted voluntarily. Although we are not to measure non-Adventists (Gentiles) by our standards, they will try to measure us by theirs. The beast will try to force our obedience to his rule for 42 months as this verse says.

(3–4) "And I will give power unto my two witnesses, and they shall prophesy a thousand two hundred and three score days, clothed in sackcloth. These are the two olive trees, and the two candlesticks standing before the God of the earth." This is God's answer to the attack on

Revelation 11

the "holy city," God's (SDA) church, and His law, during this same 42 months, or 1260 days. "I will give power," He says, coming to our aid.

To identify the two witnesses a marginal reference takes you to Zech. 4:3. "These empty themselves into the golden bowls, which represent the hearts of the living messengers of God, who bear the word of the Lord to the people in warnings and entreaties. The Word itself must be as represented, the golden oil, emptied from the two olive trees that stand by the Lord of the whole earth. This is the baptism of the Holy Spirit by fire. This will open the soul of unbelievers to conviction. The wants of the soul can be met only by the working of the Holy Spirit of God. Man can do nothing of himself to satisfy the longings and meet the aspirations of the heart." (4BC 1180)

In a nutshell, the golden bowls are the hearts of the believers who receive the golden oil from the two olive trees. The two olive trees are the Word of God (Old and New testaments) called the two witnesses in verse three above. These prophetic portions are Dan. and Rev. since they are said to prophesy. This is the baptism of the Holy Spirit by fire," Ellen White says. It brings conviction, and without conviction nothing happens. We will know more about these two witnesses after we have a clearer picture of last events.

As soon as the beast receives power, he attacks the saints on the Sabbath of God, to demand worship on Sunday, and God sends the Holy Spirit on all believers. "And it shall come to pass in the last days, saith God, I will pour out of my Spirit upon all flesh: and your sons and your daughters shall prophesy, and your young men shall see visions, and your old men shall dream dreams." (Acts 2:17) This is the Loud Cry and Latter Rain (1260 day) period.

"And at the commencement of the time of trouble, we were filled with the Holy Ghost as we went forth and proclaimed the Sabbath more fully." (EW 33) But a footnote here refers to p. 85 where she explains, "The commencement of that time of trouble, here mentioned, does not refer

Bible Facts About the 144,000

to the time when the plagues shall begin to be poured out, but to a short period (1260 days) just before they are poured out, while Christ is in the sanctuary ... at that time the "latter rain" or refreshing from the presence of the Lord, will come to give power to the loud voice of the third angel."

This makes it clear that when the beast power enforces Sunday during these 1260 days, the 144000 will receive power to prophesy (the close of probation 1260 days later) and to proclaim the Sabbath more fully. And "This is the baptism of the Holy Spirit by fire," the Latter Rain period. (See also EW page 86, top.)

Notice that this power to prophesy is given only during the 1260 days. It is given the very day the beast receives power from the state to demand worship on Sunday. We count from that day, 1260 days to the close of probation. Dan.11:27 says: "And both these kings' hearts shall be to do mischief, and they shall speak lies at one table; but it shall not prosper; for yet the end shall be at the time appointed." Who are these two kings? Revelation tells us, for these are the two powers who work together "to make WAR with the saints" (Rev. 13:7) "and cause that as many as would not worship the image of the beast should be killed." (Rev. 13:15) "the beast ... shall make WAR against them, and shall overcome them, and KILL them," (Rev. 11:7) "These shall make WAR with the Lamb, and the Lamb shall overcome them." (Rev.17:14) How does He overcome them? "And after three days and an half the Spirit of life from God entered into them, (the saints) and they stood upon their feet; and great fear fell upon them." (the undertakers which saw them in their glorified bodies!) "And they heard a great voice from heaven saying unto them, Come up hither. And they ascended up to heaven in a cloud; and their enemies beheld them," saw them go up. (Rev. 11:11–12) So He overcomes them by returning His whole army (144000) to life, and taking them up to heaven.

This war shouldn't be any secret. I capitalized the word WAR in the places in Revelation that spell it out in plain sight for everyone to see and believe. Dan.11:27 refers to this WAR as "mischief." Why is it called mischief? Because if it were done to the wicked, it would be called "punishment." They deserve it. But the righteous don't deserve it, so it's called mischief. "But it shall not prosper." Why? Because "the Lamb shall overcome them: for He is Lord of lords, and King of kings, and they that are with him are called, and chosen and faithful." (Rev. 17:14) He returns His saints to life, and whisks them off to heaven out of reach. This closes probation, and the plagues follow immediately. Rev. 11:6 says, "These (144000) have power to shut heaven, (close probation) that it rain not (no saving grace) in the days of their prophecy, (the next 1335 days) and (they) have power over waters to turn them to blood, and to smite the earth with all plagues, (all seven of them) as often as they will," or in their exact order. In the very next verses the 144000 are all killed, return to life, and ascend to heaven. This closes probation, because even the wicked see that it pays to worship God now; no faith required, and "whatsoever is not of faith is sin." (Rom. 14:23,) and the plagues are poured out at the close of probation.

(5–6) "And if any man will hurt them, fire proceedeth out of their mouth, and devoureth their enemies: and if any man will hurt them, he must in this manner be killed. These have power to shut heaven, that it rain not in the days of their prophecy: and have power over waters to turn them to blood, and to smite the earth with all plagues, as often as they will." In verses 3 and 4 we saw that the two witnesses represent the Old and New Testaments, or more precisely, Daniel and Revelation, showing us how and when probation will close, followed quickly by the plagues. Thus "if any man will hurt them, fire proceedeth out of their mouth, and devoureth their enemies." What kind of fire? Obviously not the kind of fire the Holy Spirit baptized the saints with in verse 3. But this fire devours their enemies. And since it is out of the mouth of the witnesses, it is another kind of symbolic fire, or it would burn their mouths. This fire means the plagues, which are brought on by closing probation. "and if any man will hurt them, he must in this manner be killed." The witnesses give the three angels' messages. To disregard their warning against the worship of the beast is to fall into the plagues automatically. Thus it is quite literally out of the mouths of the two witnesses above.

(7) "And when they shall have finished their testimony, the beast that ascendeth out of the bottomless pit shall make war against them, and shall overcome them, and kill them." Near the end of the 1260 days, the "beast" kills the 144000 who have finished giving the three angels' messages. I know this is contrary to what we have been taught, but God must know the meaning of the word "kill," and we have no right to think he was mistaken in using it here. But you needn't take my word for it, because it is very easy to prove that it is the 144000 who are killed.

Speaking of the 144000, Rev. 14:5 says they are "faultless before the throne of God." Therefore Satan cannot hold them in his power, nor induce them to sin. Rev. 12:11 says: "and they loved not their lives unto the death." Rev. 13:15 says: "as many as would not worship the image of the beast should be killed." The 144000 do not worship this image, so they are killed. If they did worship him, they could not be said to be faultless. The 144000 are the only ones who dare to make war with the beast. A war is not just a difference of opinion. It is not war unless somebody gets killed. In Rev. 11:7 the beast kills those who refuse to worship him. But they come back to life and ascend to heaven. (vss. 11–12) This springs the trap on Satan for murdering innocent people, and proves the 144000 are the victims of Rev. 11:7. So we have it.

(8–10) "And their dead bodies shall lie in the street of the great city, which spiritually is called Sodom and Egypt, where also our Lord was crucified. And they of the people and kindreds and tongues and nations shall see their dead bodies three days and an half, and shall not suffer their dead bodies to be put in graves. And they that

Revelation 11

dwell upon the earth shall rejoice over them, and make merry, and shall send gifts one to another: because these two prophets tormented them that dwell on the earth." Notice how their dead bodies are mentioned three times. After they are killed they are not even given a proper burial in graves because their killers want to be sure everyone will have a chance to "see their dead bodies" and know what happens to folks who refuse to worship the beast. In verse 8, Sodom and Egypt are to be taken symbolically, as it says. But the dead bodies and graves are not to be taken that way. It could not be put any plainer if it were right out of the local morning paper. Every Adventist should know that God knows the end from the beginning, and that these three verses could mean your dead body if you are ready to die for your faith. If so, you will be resurrected to ascend three days later. If not, you will die in the plagues according to verse 5 above. Either way you ought to study these things for yourself.

"Satan watches to catch away every impression that would make them (us) wise unto salvation, and the time of trouble will find them (us) unready." (unless we wake up quickly) (GC594) Every SDA is well aware that the ten virgins of the parable all slept until "at midnight there was a cry made, Behold, the bridegroom cometh: go ye out to meet him." To believe, and to follow any man, or group of people, contrary to the Bible, is to have a false Christ. You are saved by following God and His truth. Follow the Bible as it reads.

Whatever you do, don't plan on a deathbed repentance at the last minute, because there is no such thing as deathbed repentance for Seventh-day Adventists! Why not? Because "Character cannot be changed when Christ comes, nor just as a man dies. A few resolves, a few tears, will never reverse a guilty past life nor blot out of the books of heaven the transgressions, the willful, knowing sin of those who have had the previous light of truth, and can explain the Scriptures to others while sin and iniquity are drunk up like stolen waters." (TM 430)

Bible Facts About the 144,000

We do not become "new creatures" by tears and resolves at the last minute, but by agonizing in prayer to God, pleading for His mercy and grace for victory over sin in our lives. Sanctification is the work of a life time that cannot be faked. It is a life and death struggle for which there is no substitute other than the love and mercy of Christ. "The kingdom of heaven suffereth violence, and the violent take it by force." (Matt. 11:12) The violent are the very elect who "are arrayed in fine linen, clean and white: for the fine linen is the righteousness of saints." (Rev. 19:8)

When prisoners are released, they are often given a certain period of probationary time to prove whether they have learned self control, and are safe to mingle in an unprotected society. Smokers are not confident of victory until they can say "I have no more uncontrollable hankering." The same with any bad habit. Even our mental habits. So we have to be completely free of all sin for a reasonable length of time BEFORE probation closes, to prove ourselves to God that we are free of sin. "I can do all things through Christ which strentheneth me" Paul says in Phil. 4:13, and this is our only means of salvation. It must be done during the Early Rain period, and can't be done without His special help. The 144000 will have proven themselves free of every besetment for a reasonable probationary period before the Early Rain ends, and it ends the first day of the Latter Rain. Nobody is to know that day, which comes without warning, "like a thief in the night." All this will be easy to prove as you read on. The 144000 are filled with the Holy Ghost at Acts 2:17, on the first day of the Latter Rain. They are the only ones who can learn 'that song' (victory over every besetment) for a reasonable time before that day. The Early Rain is the growing season, and very peaceful. The crop reaches perfection (fully ripe) and waits briefly at peace for the harvest days to begin. The grim reaper holds "in his hand a sharp sickle" waiting for the loud voice telling him to "Thrust in thy sickle, and reap: for the time is come for thee to reap; for the harvest of the earth is ripe." (Rev.

Revelation 11

14:15) "Ripe" means "faultless before the throne of God. (vs 5) This "sharp sickle" is the close of probation for church members; so sharp it works infallibly. The Spirit is poured out on the wise virgins, and withdrawn from the foolish virgins; the door is shut between them on the first day of the (1260) Latter Rain period. "And at the commencement of the time of trouble, we were filled with the Holy Ghost … .The commencement of that time of trouble, here mentioned, does not refer to the time when the plagues shall be poured out, but to a short period (1260 days) just before they are poured out, while Christ is in the sanctuary." (ER 85)

(11) "And after three days and an half the Spirit of life from God entered into them, and they stood upon their feet; and great fear fell upon them which saw them." Three days and a half is about the limit to leave dead bodies lying around where they died, especially in warm country, and expect the undertakers to handle them. So the touch of the undertakers is the moment God chooses to return them to life, right in the undertakers' hands! This also assures every one of God's saints an expert witness to their return to life. "And great fear fell on them" (the undertakers.) Why? Are undertakers afraid of dead bodies? No. Are they afraid of live ones? Then why such "great fear?" The very next verse says these saints ascended to heaven, and "flesh and blood" cannot enter heaven. Only glorified bodies enter heaven. So the "great fear" indicates these bodies not only came alive unexpectedly, but were blindingly radiant to sinful eyes!

We need to understand the difference between sinful flesh, and a glorified body. When Moses came off the mount from communing with God his face shone. So much so that it was extremely uncomfortable for his friends, and he wore a veil. (Ex. 34:29–35) But if Moses' whole body had been glorified, His friends would have been stricken as dead men, like when the angel rolled away the stone at Jesus' tomb. Only glorified bodies go to heaven.

Bible Facts About the 144,000

(12) "And they heard a great voice from heaven saying unto them, Come up hither. And they ascended up to heaven in a cloud; and their enemies beheld them." Not only do the wicked witness their return to life, but also their ascension to heaven and out of Satan's reach as well. Since the 144000 are in heaven during the plagues and return with Jesus when He comes, (Jude 14) they are entirely separate from the great multitude of Rev. 7:9.

"And Jesus would be honored by translating, without seeing death, the faithful, waiting ones who had so long expected him." (EW 283) This is the statement so mistakenly used for the notion that the 144000 would be translated without seeing death. It doesn't even mention the 144000! The 144000 are the "firstfruits" of the two part harvest. How could they be the "firstfruits" unless they precede the main harvest? E.W. 283 means the "great multitude" of Rev. 7:9.

THE FIRSTFRUITS

Speaking of the 144000, Rev.14:4 says: 'These were redeemed from among men, being the firstfruits unto God and to the Lamb." That they ascend before probation closes is evident from this because it says "they are the firstfruits unto God and to the Lamb." Jesus is still the Lamb (intercessor) until probation closes. They ascend at Rev. 11:12, but probation doesn't close until vs. 15. Between verses 12 and 15 something extremely important happens while Jesus is still the Lamb and still interceding. But we need to know more about "the great multitude" of Rev. 7:9 first. They are the main part of the harvest, of which the 144000 are only the firstfruits. Many millions of people (saints of God in every sense of the word,) GREET Jesus when He comes, but the 144000 return WITH Him when He comes, as we saw in Jude 14.

"During His ministry, Jesus had raised the dead to life. He had raised the son of the widow of Nain, and the ruler's daughter and Lazarus. But these were not clothed with immortality. After they were raised, they were still subject to death. But those who came forth from the grave at Christ's resurrection were raised to everlasting life. They ascended with Him as trophies of His victory over death and the grave. These, said Christ, are no longer the captives of Satan; I have REDEEMED them. I have brought them from the grave as the FIRSTFRUITS of my power, to be with Me where I am, nevermore to see death or experience sorrow." (DA 786) Redeemed and glorified are practically synonymous.

Let's point out a few obvious facts here. Three people were raised "still subject to death." In other words, they were not raised with glorified bodies to ascend to heaven, but with the same mortal bodies, unchanged. These were not said to be "redeemed" nor free from death and sorrow. Neither were they called trophies, nor "firistfruits of my power." Christ was present at the raising of these three, and with Moses.

Elijah raised the widow's son back from the dead. (I Kings 17:17–24) Peter raised up Dorcus after she had died. (Acts 9:36–41) Paul brought Eutychus back to life. (Acts 20:9–11) God can give anybody the power to raise the dead. He gives this power not because they are more worthy, but only if it serves His purposes under the circumstances. Likewise, when He needs 144000 to do some special work, He empowers them. Not because they are superior beings, but because of their faith in Jesus to do as He wills. I don't mean to belittle the 144000, but to show that their power is all from Jesus, not in themselves.

NOTES ON MATTHEW 24:45–51

Matt.24 is a lengthy discourse on last events and the return of Jesus. Verses 45–51 may seem like comparatively mild and harmless words, yet they climax the whole chapter about His Second Coming. He stresses the lesson of these six verses by adding, "there shall be weeping and gnashing of teeth." Whose teeth? His servant's teeth. These six verses caution His servants, and are obviously very important. Let's study them in view of what we have learned so far.

"Who then is a faithful and wise servant, whom his lord hath made ruler over his household, to give them meat in due season? Blessed is that servant, whom his lord when he cometh shall find so doing. Verily I say unto you, that he shall make him ruler over all his goods.
But and if that evil servant shall say in his heart, My lord delayeth his coming; And shall begin to smite his fellow servants, and to eat and drink with the drunken; the lord of that servant shall come in a day when he looketh not for him, and in an hour that he is not aware of, and shall cut him asunder, and appoint him his portion with the hypocrites: there shall be weeping and gnashing of teeth."(Matt. 24;45–51)

"The language of the Bible should be explained according to its obvious meaning, unless a symbol or figure is employed." (GC 599) This is the rule, so first we need to decide whether to take this passage literally or symbolically. Should we consider the "meat in due season" as real beef, or as a symbol of spiritual food? And should we expect to see our fellow church members going around hitting one another and getting stone drunk because they think Jesus is slow in coming? Probably not, so let's try it the other way and apply it spiritually.

First let's notice that one servant is called "blessed" while the other is called "evil" yet both are called servants (church members) for those outside His household don't even pretend to serve Him. Also notice that they are considered good or evil depending on their attitude toward the time of His coming. See how many times time is mentioned: in due season; (vs 45) when he cometh; (vs 46) delayeth his coming; (vs 48) come in a day; and in an hour (vs 50). In fact the whole of Matt.24 relates to the time of His coming. It seems quite clear then, that Jesus is distinguishing the good and evil by their attitude toward the time of His Coming. Those who "give meat in due season" are those who know the time and share it at the proper time regardless of the consequences. Those who deny His Coming, smite their fellow servants, and drink with the drunken. In a spiritual sense, "smiting" could indicate they vote to disfellowship those who prophesy His Coming. To prophesy the exact time is a real no no in the Adventist Church even though God Himself makes it known to us by setting up the beast power. "Drinking with the drunken" must mean they are "made drunk by the wine of her fornication" (Rev. 17:2) They worship the beast to avoid death. (Rev. 13:8 and 15)

The cause of this conflict is not in whether or not the Bible is clear regarding the time, but because of some confusion as to how it should be read. When we read something in the Bible, should we ask if anyone else believes it, or should we take God at His word? If my friends don't believe it, does God expect me to? If the pastor or the commentaries explain a text away unconvincingly, should I just let it drop? Paul said, "Immediately I conferred not with flesh and blood. Neither went I up to Jerusalem to them which were apostles before me." (Gal.1:16–17) Thus Paul did not let flesh and blood take precedence over God's word and Spirit. Neither did Abraham when asked to sacrifice his son. The Bible says, "Abraham believed God, and it was counted unto him for righteousness." (Rom.4:3) Never mind that I'm only a piano tuner, just watch out that I don't try to twist, or misapply a Scripture or a symbol to try to make God say something He never intended. When God swears the

Notes On Matthew 24:45–51

most powerful oath in the Bible you'd better pay attention to God, not me. Abraham wouldn't just laugh it off; neither should we.

"Trust in the Lord with all thine heart; and lean not unto thine own understanding." (Prov. 3:5) In other words, don't even confer with your own blood, but trust God and obey His word. "All thy children shall be taught of the Lord." (Isaiah 54:13) "Every man therefore that hath heard, and hath learned of the Father, cometh unto me." (John 6:45) "The anointing which ye have received of Him abideth in you, and ye need not that any man teach you." (1 John 2:27) "And they shall not teach every man his neighbor, and every man his brother, saying, Know the Lord: for all shall know me, from the least to the greatest." (Heb. 8:11)

Even if one were born in a cave and never saw a light until fully grown up, he could instantly detect the light of a candle unless he had been born blind. And if he lived all his life by candlelight he could easily see by a more modern electric light, unless he were prejudiced and closed his eyes. The same works with the truth.

By this analogy, we should be willing to accept the death of the 144000 as present truth directly from the Bible. Before Ellen White's day, people were guided by the Holy Spirit to read the Bible for present truth as history unfolded throughout the centuries. There is no reason to believe we should not be free to do the same after her death in matters she was not shown. Especially when she herself said: "We have only the glimmerings of the rays of the light that is yet to come to us," (1SM 401) and only from the Bible.

Most Adventists don't realize that God "locked" Ellen White's mind for 2 or 3 years so she couldn't understand the Scriptures that our main doctrines are based on! "Many of our people do not realize how firmly the foundation of our faith has been laid." she says. "My husband, Elder Joseph Bates, Father Piece, Elder Edson and others who were keen, noble and true, were among those who, after the passing of the time in 1844, searched for the truth as for hidden treasure. I met with them, and we studied and prayed earnestly. Often we remained together until late at night, and some times through the entire night, praying for light and studying the Word. Again and again these brethren came together to study the Bible, in order that they might know its meaning, and be prepared to teach it with power. When they came to the point in their study where they said, "We can do nothing more," the Spirit of the Lord would come upon me, I would be taken off in vision, and a clear explanation of the passages we had been studying would be given me, with instruction as to how we were to labor and teach effectively. Thus, light was given that helped us understand the Scriptures in regard to Christ, His mission, and His priesthood. A line of truth extending from that time to the time when we should enter the city of God, was made plain to me, and I gave to others the instruction that the Lord had given me.

"During this whole time I could not understand the reasoning of the brethren. My mind was locked, as it were, and I could not comprehend the meaning of the Scriptures we were studying. This was one of the greatest sorrows of my life. I was in this condition of mind until all the principle points of our faith were made clear to our minds, in harmony with the Word of God. The brethren knew that when not in vision, I could not understand these matters, and they accepted as light direct from heaven the revelations given.

"For two or three years my mind continued to be locked to an understanding of the Scriptures. In the course of our labors, my husband and I visited Father Andrews, who was suffering intensely with inflammatory rheumatism. We prayed for him. I laid my hands on his head, and said, "Father Andrews, the Lord Jesus maketh thee whole." He was healed instantly. He got up, and walked about the room, praising God and saying, "I never saw it on this wise before. Angels of God are in this room." The glory of the Lord was revealed. Light seemed to shine all though the house, and an angel's hand was laid on my head. From that time

Notes On Matthew 24:45–51

to this I have been able to understand the Word of God." (ISM pp. 206–207)

The point is, God expects us (common people) to dig out all new light (present truth) from the Bible itself. Even if she were with us today, the common people must study the Scriptures "as for hidden treasure." Anyone reading honestly and reasonably, and believing God at face value will arrive at the identical conclusions you are reading here. All we have to do is let God lead where He will without dragging our feet nor trying to improve or change anything in the Bible. God cannot be our God if we doubt Him in any way. Eve doubted Him in Eden. "These are they which follow the Lamb whithersoever he goeth." (Rev. 14:4) God sees the end from the beginning. "Present truth" is FRESH and straight from the Bible. Otherwise it may be stale or tainted by outside contamination. The manna (bread from heaven) got stale over night. Even though it was from heaven it had to be FRESH to be nourishing. Eternal truth and present truth are not the same whether from the Bible, or from the pen of inspiration. Present truth gets stale, because it is subject to time. Eternal truth is not subject to time. It never changes, and it is always true.

We have already noted that when Christ comes, there will be only two classes to greet Him, those found written in the book of life, and those who are not. We have also seen how the World Sunday Law causes the final separation. But before this there is a separation within God's true church whether or not they have oil in their lamps. At midnight a cry is made, "Behold, the bridegroom cometh; go ye out to meet him." (Matt. 25:6) Until this time there seemed to be no difference between them. Yet most of them were lost. How could they miss by such a small margin? They were already in the true church. But because they were foolish, it says. The dictionary defines "foolish" as "marked by, or proceeding from folly. Absurd; Ridiculous." "They that were foolish took their lamps, and took no oil with them." (Matt. 25:3) A very foolish mistake! They all had the prophecy:

43

Bible Facts About the 144,000

they were a church of prophecy which was to light the way ahead like a lamp. But they didn't believe it. If we don't believe what we see, it's the same as blindness. And not perceiving the time, we may never bother to perfect our characters. We may keep putting it off thinking we will have time later. But when "later" came they were shut out and couldn't get back in. "Afterward came also the other virgins, saying, Lord, Lord, open to us. But he answered and said, "Verily I say unto you, I know you not." (Matt. 25:11–12) Fatal words! For relative trifles we may forfeit trillions of years of total bliss! All of eternity! Even while Jesus is still interceding in the sanctuary above, He cannot forgive our sins unless we ask Him. Neither can He cleanse us unless we ask Him, and obey Him. And if we neglect or renounce light and truth, we literally shut the door as in Noah's day. For all practical purposes the shut door doctrine is the same as the close of probation.

"There was a shut door in Noah's day. There was at that time a withdrawal of the Spirit of God from the sinful race that perished in the waters of the Flood. God Himself gave the shut-door message to Noah:

"My spirit shall not always strive with man, for that he also is flesh: yet his days shall be an hundred and twenty years" (Gen. 6:3)

There was a shut door in the days of Abraham. Mercy ceased to plead with the inhabitants of Sodom, and all but Lot, with his wife and two daughters, were consumed by the fire sent down from heaven.

There was a shut door in Christ's day. The Son of God declared to the unbelieving Jews of that generation, "Your house is left unto you desolate" (Matt. 23: 38).

Looking down the stream of time to the last days, the same infinite power proclaimed through John: "These things saith he that is holy, he that is true, he that hath the key of David, he that openeth, and no man shutteth; and shutteth, and no man openeth" (Rev. 3:7).

Notes On Matthew 24:45–51

I was shown in vision, and I still believe, that there was a shut door in 1844. All who saw the light of the first and second angels' messages and rejected that light, were left in darkness. And those who accepted it and received the Holy Spirit which attended the proclamation of the message from heaven, and who afterward renounced their faith and pronounced their experience a delusion, thereby rejected the Spirit of God, and it no longer pleaded with them.

Those who did not see the light, had not the guilt of its rejection. It was only the class who had despised the light from heaven that the Spirit of God could not reach. And this class included, as I have stated, both those who refused to accept the message when it was presented to them, and also those who, having received it, afterward renounced their faith. These might have a form of godliness, and profess to be followers of Christ, but having no living connection with God, they would be taken captive by the delusions of Satan." (1SM 63–64)

This is how probation closes for the church before Jesus leaves the sanctuary in heaven. When we accept Jesus as our Saviour and are baptized, our sins are forgiven. If we died that very minute we would be saved like the thief on the cross. But baptism doesn't destroy the old nature, and we can be tempted to sin again. Only the 144000 actually learn perfect self control of mind and body, reflecting the image of Jesus fully under all possible temptation, with no further need of divine intercession. The rest of the church is in the Laodicean condition, neither cold nor hot, and the Holy Spirit cannot be poured out on them on the first day of the 1260 day Latter Rain period, "and the door was shut." (Matt. 25:10)

Thus a Laodicean is a baptized church member dallying on Satan's ground, rejecting known light, and crucifying the Saviour afresh right up to the day that "I shall come on thee as a thief in the night" on the day the Holy Spirit is poured out the first day of the 1260 days, and we will not know that day in advance. Thus no Adventist

45

knows the day the door will shut and close probation for them. The wise virgins (SDA's) don't make a business of living in sin presumptuously. They are ready and free of sin, safely awaiting the "shut door" close of probation before the 1260 days begin the Latter Rain period. Thus we are never to know the definite time for the outpouring of the Holy Spirit, which is a shut door type close of probation and this book cannot tell you that day. That day is sealed up until the very day the Holy Spirit is poured out. Counting from the first day it is poured out to the ascension of the 144000 is 1260 days. Jesus leaves the sanctuary to greet them in heaven, and that closes probation to all forever. Then there will be 1335 days of plagues to the Second Coming.

Please notice that to reject a heavenly truth is to shut the door, closing probation to that person, or persons. It is like spurning the Holy Ghost, or blasphemy. It is the unpardonable sin as explained in Matt. 12:31–32. Also the foolish virgins' lack of oil.

William Miller's work was based on the 2300 days of Dan. 8:14 and on the oath of Rev. 10:6 saying: "And the angel ... sware by him that liveth for ever ... that there should be time no longer." God moved him to preach the end of the world in 1844. And those who rejected that light were shut out in darkness.

This work is based on a similar oath of God in Dan. 12:7 saying: "And sware by him that liveth for ever ... all these things shall be finished." This time it will be the real end of the world! Anyone God cannot reach with this light will not be reached at all, and the door will be shut for the last time. Thus as soon as you read this book the sealing time has begun for you. "The sealing time is very short, (after you read this) and will soon be over. Now is the time, while the four angels are holding the four winds, to make our calling and election sure." (EW 58) How? By overcoming every sin.

Now let's go to 2T p. 604 for a backstage view of how God works to help us do that. My comments in brackets.

46

Notes On Matthew 24:45–51

"On the night of April 30, 1871, I retired to rest much depressed in spirits. For three months I had been in a state of great discouragement. I had frequently prayed in anguish of spirit for relief. I had implored help and strength from God, that I might rise above the heavy discouragements that were paralyzing my faith and hope, and unfitting me for usefulness. (She was 43, and, "In addition to the menopause through which she was passing, she suffered much from a painful ... growing cancer in the breast." p. 329, The Progressive Years. If she wrestled with God for three months for His help, can we expect Him to be any easier on us? And remember, He loves us. He doesn't do it for the fun of it, but for our own good.) That night I had a dream which made a very happy impression upon my mind. I dreamed that I was attending an important meeting at which a large company were assembled.

Many were bowed before God in earnest prayer, and they seemed to be burdened. They were importuning the Lord for special light. A few seemed to be in agony of spirit; their feelings were intense; with tears they were crying aloud for help and light. Our most prominent brethren were engaged in this most impressive scene. Brother A was prostrated upon the floor, apparently in deep distress. (wrestling with God?) His wife was sitting among a company of indifferent scorners. She looked as though she desired all to understand that she scorned those who were thus humiliating themselves.

"I dreamed that the Spirit of the Lord came upon me, and I arose amid cries and prayers, and said: The Spirit of the Lord is upon me. I feel urged to say to you that you must commence to work individually for yourselves. You are looking to God and desiring Him to do the work for you which He has left for you to do. If you will do the work for yourselves which you know that you ought to do, then God will help you when you need help. You have left undone the very things which God has left for you to do. You have been calling upon God to do your work. (What work? This work. Listen to her.) Had you followed

Bible Facts About the 144,000

the light which He has given you, then He would cause more light to shine upon you; but while you neglect the counsels, warnings, and reproofs that have been given, how can you expect God to give you more light and blessings to neglect and despise? God is not a man; He will not be trifled with. (Obedience is love. Disobedience is not. Obedience is worship. How can we worship God and not do as He says? Courting a woman is finding out what she likes and doing it. Same idea. But isn't "works" legalism? Yes. It's like courting her as a business deal (cold heartedly) without love. Does she have to tell him to stop smoking, drinking, and gambling? Not at all. To do these things before he fell in love would be "works," but suddenly just to know her is all it takes. "Therefore if any man be in Christ, he is a new creature: old things are passed away; behold, all things are become new." Same thing. So …)

"I took the precious Bible and surrounded it with the several "Testimonies for the Church," given for the people of God. Here, said I, the cases of nearly all are met. The sins they are to shun are pointed out. The counsel that they desire can be found here, given for other cases situated similarly to themselves. God has been pleased to give you line upon line and precept upon precept. But there are not many of you that really know what is contained in the Testimonies. You are not familiar with the Scriptures. If you had made God's word your study, with a desire to reach the Bible standard and attain to Christian perfection, you would not have needed the Testimonies. It is because you have neglected to acquaint yourselves with God's inspired Book that He has sought to reach you by simple, direct testimonies, calling your attention to the words of inspiration which you had neglected to obey, and urging you to fashion your lives in accordance with its pure and elevated teachings.

"The Lord designs to warn you, to reprove, to counsel, through the testimonies given, and to impress your minds with the importance of the truth of His word. The written testimonies are not to give new light, but to impress vividly

Notes On Matthew 24:45–51

upon the heart the truths of inspiration already revealed. Man's duty to God and to his fellow man has been distinctly specified in God's word; yet but few of you are obedient to the light given. Additional truth is not brought out; but God has through the Testimonies simplified the great truths already given and in His own chosen way brought them before the people to awaken and impress the mind with them, that all may be without excuse.

"Pride, self-love, selfishness, hatred, envy, and jealousy have beclouded the perceptive powers, and the truth, which would make you wise unto salvation, has lost its power to charm and control the mind. The very essential principles of godliness are not understood because there is not a hungering and thirsting for Bible knowledge, purity of heart, and holiness of life. The Testimonies are not to belittle the word of God, but to exalt it and attract minds to it, that the beautiful simplicity of truth may impress all.

"I said further: As the word of God is walled in with these books and pamphlets, so has God walled you in with reproofs, counsel, warnings and encouragements. Here you are crying before God, in the anguish of your souls, for more light. I am authorized from God to tell you that not another ray of light through the Testimonies will shine upon your pathway until you make a practical use of the light already given. The Lord has walled you about with light; but you have not appreciated the light; you have trampled upon it. While some have despised the light, others have neglected it, or followed it but indifferently. A few have set their hearts to obey the light which God has been pleased to give them.

"Some that have received special warnings through testimonies have forgotten in a few weeks the reproof given. The testimonies to some have been several times repeated, but they have not thought them of sufficient importance to be carefully heeded. They have been to them like idle tales. Had they regarded the light given they would have avoided losses and trials which they think are hard and severe." (2T 604–606) But it goes on for three more pages! So if what you are reading here about the 144000 and last day events doesn't stir your blood, what else do you expect God to show you from the Bible? He certainly can't come to you in Person, because you would evaporate like a drop of dew in a furnace. All He dare use is the Bible and the still small voice of the Holy Spirit.

We began this chapter with a closer look at the warning in the last verses of Matt. 24:45 and on, "Therefore be ye also ready," and "there shall be weeping and gnashing of teeth." We all wrestle with God for His blessing, as Jacob did, and God has given us the "Testimonies" for even more help with the details of salvation. "How shall we escape, if we neglect so great salvation?" (Heb. 2:3) "Yet but few of you are obedient to the light given." That was in 1871! And in the second of nine volumes of the Testimonies. She wrote seven more that we "neglect and despise!"

For instance, in those days they prayed "in agony of spirit" "crying aloud for help and light." Now, even though we are so much worse off than they were, this would be unthinkable nowadays. We not only neglect the "Testimonies" but are so insensitive to our need of them, we hardly give them a second thought. The pastor almost never quotes from them, and we certainly don't go prostrate on the floor in agony of spirit about it! So then what? "The lord of that servant shall come in a day when he looketh not for him, and in an hour he is not aware of, and shall cut him asunder, and appoint him his portion with the hypocrites: there shall be weeping and gnashing of teeth." (Matt.24:50,51) Why? Because they don't care.

"Some, I saw, did not participate in this work of agonizing and pleading. They were not resisting the darkness around them, and it shut them in like a thick cloud. The angels of God left these and went to the aid of the earnest praying ones. I saw angels of God hasten to the assistance of all who were struggling with all their power to resist the evil angels and trying to help themselves by

Notes On Matthew 24:45–51

calling upon God with perseverance. (We are powerless, until we ask God.) But His angels left those who made no effort to help themselves, and I lost sight of them." How terrible! She is talking about Seventh Day Adventists in the last days right here, (you and I) because I copied this from "The Shaking Time" (EW p.270)

JOHN 10:16 AND REV. 18:4

If you are a Seventh-day Adventist you will probably agree that the Millerite movement was inspired of God. Believers at that time were separated from the formal churches against their will for believing in a date for the exact end of time. Our church sprung up from these believers. Receiving special instruction to free them from long time errors, they were to warn the world of the judgment to come, and to prepare a people for heaven. "Study Revelation in connection with Daniel, for history will be repeated." (TM 116) If history is to be repeated, would you agree that the 144000 will be separated from the main body of the Seventh-day Adventist Church, similar to the believers in 1844 for believing the exact time also? If not, do you have a satisfactory explanation for the Laodiceans being "spewed out?" Especially since this means "to vomit?" (See Strong's Concordance) And would you agree that the ten virgins of the parable, and the Laodiceans, represent the same church in the last days, and that the midnight cry is what separates the believers from unbelievers; the ready from the unready?

If you do object to the premises above, you may be thinking of this: "The church may appear as about to fall, but it does not fall. It remains, while the sinners in Zion will be sifted out; the chaff separated from the precious wheat. This is a terrible ordeal, but nevertheless it must take place. None but those who have been overcoming by the blood of the Lamb and by the word of their testimony will be found with the loyal and true, without spot or stain of sin, without guile in their mouths." (2SM 380) Thus the inevitable separation, but the whole church doesn't fall. Gideon had only 300 tried and true warriors out of 32000. This time it will be 144000 out of many million members separating the ready from the unready.

John 10:16 and Rev. 18:4

The question is, what constitutes the church? Is it the organization, or the people that go to heaven if found written in the Book? It is the people. And when the work is finished the organization will have served its purpose and no longer needed. The organization is only a tool, like a threshing machine, to prepare the wheat permanently. It doesn't go to heaven; only the people go to heaven.

Therefore, the test is not whether their names are on the church registry, but whether or not they are faultless before the throne of God, and not blotted out of the book of life of the Lamb. Thus she describes them in almost the same words as Rev. 14:5, "And in their mouth was found no guile: for they are without fault before the throne of God." So the 144000 must be the true church of the last generation, and the Laodiceans must be the foolish virgins which are "spewed out" several million strong. They are not "spewed out" of the Laodicean church, but out of the mouth of God; out of the book of life of the Lamb. Only the 144000 who reflect the image of Jesus fully, and are ready to ascend to heaven in the special resurrection, are saved, as we will see. The whole Jewish nation was spewed out of His mouth, and now only Jews whose names are found written in the book of life can hope to be saved.

God is no respecter of persons. We aren't saved because we are Jews or SDA's, but only if our names are found in the Book. When is our name entered in the book of life? When we accept Jesus as our Saviour at baptism. And if we learn to reflect the image of Jesus fully, thus abiding in Jesus at our death, or at His Coming, it will not be blotted out. If we reject any light the Holy Spirit shows us, we cannot be led to heaven. We have left the path of truth.

Perhaps we should clarify one point right here in case some may wonder what it takes to keep our names in the book of life. Chapter 3 of 2SM is entitled "The 'Holy Flesh' Doctrine." Regarding this "fanaticism" Ellen White said, "The teaching given in regard to what is termed "holy flesh" is an error. All may now obtain holy hearts, but it is not correct to claim in this life to have holy flesh. The apostle Paul declares, "I know that in me (that is, in my flesh,) dwelleth no good thing" (Romans 7:18). To those who have tried so hard to obtain by faith so-called holy flesh, I would say, You cannot obtain it. Not a soul of you has holy flesh now. No human being on earth has holy flesh. It is an impossibility." (2SM 32) I think it is safe to say that only a glorified body is holy flesh, and is a miraculous change bestowing us with the robe of light to withstand the glories of heaven. B-I-B-L-E means Bible Instruction Before Leaving Earth, entitling us to the change. "When human beings receive holy flesh, they will not remain on the earth, but will be taken to heaven. (as at Rev. 11:12) While sin is forgiven in this life, its results are not now wholly removed. It is at His coming that Christ is to "change our vile body, that it may be fashioned like unto his glorious body." (2SM 33)

In a nutshell then, let's sum up so far like this: there will be a National Sunday Law; then a World Sunday Law. The day the beast receives power to demand worship of the saints; we can count the exact time to the end: 1260 literal days to the close of probation, then 1335 days of plagues to the return of Jesus. The 144000 who believe and prophesy the exact time will be disfellowshiped for teaching other than standard doctrine. This separates them from the mother church, which has served its purpose and no longer needed. The true remnant (144000) are immediately filled with the Holy Spirit to finish their work in 1260 days.

"I saw that God had children who do not keep the Sabbath. They have not rejected the light upon it. And at the commencement of the time of trouble, we were filled with the Holy Ghost as we went forth and proclaimed the Sabbath more fully" (EW 85) The word "we" means believers, for Ellen White would never say "we" to include herself with unbelievers. So "we" means the very elect, and not the foolish virgins which were not ready to be "filled with the Holy Ghost."

John 10:16 and Rev. 18:4

Both Acts 2:17 and EW 85 refer to the outpouring of the Holy Spirit to finish the work in the last days. In 1844 the Holy Spirit was poured out on only one person, E.G.White. But here it is to be poured upon "all flesh;" all believers; the 144000. Since the 144000 are separated from the organized facilities of the church, the Holy Spirit more than makes up for this. In visions and dreams they are directed to "God's children who do not see and keep the Sabbath." And "other sheep I have, which are not of this fold: them also I must bring, and they shall hear my voice." (John 10:16) "My voice" means the truth. Anyone who will hear the truth can be led to Jesus no matter what church they are in, or out of.

Will these "other sheep" then become part of the 144000? Or do they comprise an entirely different group? The answer to this is the purpose of this chapter. Rev. 7 reveals two separate and distinct groups of God's people in the last days; the 144000 and "a great multitude, which no man could number." The 144000 are redeemed at Rev. 11:12 where they ascend to heaven. The great multitude are the rest of the harvest, gleaned as the "other sheep, not of this fold" and who wait through the plagues to be translated without seeing death at the return of Jesus. The Bible mentions nobody else ascending to heaven under any circumstances, in the last days, except the righteous dead (from all past history) who are also raised and ascend at His Coming.

The 144000, the very elect who cannot be deceived, by their very love of truth are perfecting their characters right now, for this must all be done during the Early Rain. The Latter Rain accomplishes an entirely different work, as is clearly explained in the Spirit of Prophecy books. The perfection of the 144000 renders them intolerable to nominal Adventists. Light and darkness cannot walk peaceably together and never have. When the beast receives power, and we know the exact time, it becomes the midnight cry "Behold the bridegroom cometh" because we have proof of it, and the division is made between the wise and foolish virgins of the parable. But God still has many children who would love and accept the truth if they were to hear it right. So the 144000, filled with the Holy Spirit are guided to them miraculously to teach and to show them the ways of God, just as Philip was sent to baptize the Ethiopian. (See Acts 8:26–40) All this must be done secretly under wraps, or as Rev. 11:3 says, "clothed in sackcloth," because they are quite literally saved out of the other churches, as you will see.

The 144000 will have no church records, so the names of these new converts are not formally recorded any where but in the Lamb's book of life in heaven. The 144000 were all registered in the church records. When all power is given to the beast, the church books will be confiscated in order to enforce the World Sunday Law, "and cause that as many as would not worship the image of the beast should be killed." (Rev. 13:15) But the "great multitude, which no man could number" cannot be killed because only the 144000 know who they are, and all is kept secret "clothed in sackcloth."

For this reason also, these new converts cannot leave their Sunday-keeping churches, which would be a dead giveaway. They had never heard the true Sabbath and "the everlasting gospel" before as "preached unto them that dwell on the earth" and now they must learn it under very dangerous circumstances. (See Dan. 11;31–35) Yet they love the truth more than life itself, and they hear it gladly from the 144000 saints in secrecy.

Until the 144000 reach perfection, they are still under some besetment of Satanic influence themselves, and cannot teach perfection any more than Adam could after he lost it. All who go to heaven must prove their freedom from sin, because "there shall in no wise enter into it any thing that defileth, neither whatsoever worketh abomination, or maketh a lie: but they which are written in the Lamb's book of life." (Rev. 22:27) Adam and Eve could not pass on a righteousness they had lost. Neither can the 144000 teach perfection until they have it. And "no man could learn that song but the 144000." God will not

John 10:16 and Rev. 18:4

be trifled with. The great multitude of new converts that the 144000 have been teaching all during the Latter Rain, will have to live without an Intercessor all through the 1335 days of the plagues, and this will be their probationary time to make sure they are safe to be translated to heaven at the return of Jesus. So don't plan on being saved by a death bed experience, such as the thief on the cross had. He accepted the offer of salvation as soon as he was given it. He had no probationary time left to him. But under the circumstances there would be no danger of him lacking self control later. He is beyond the reach of sin.

"Do not think that God will work a miracle to save those weak souls who cherish evil, who practice sin; or that some supernatural element will be brought into their lives, lifting them out of self into a higher sphere, where it will be comparatively easy work, without any special effort, any special fighting, without any crucifixion of self; because all who dally on Satan's ground for this to be done will perish with the evildoers." "Will you take the viper to your bosom, expecting God to put a spell upon it so it will not poison you with its venomous sting? Will you drink poison, expecting God to provide an antidote?" (TM 453, 454) Don't trifle with sin and expect to make it just under the wire. It doesn't work that way. "Behold, now is the accepted time; behold, now is the day of salvation." (2Cor. 6:2) Tomorrow you may be dead, not having the victory over every besetment, and not reflecting the image of Jesus.

But what about the great multitude of new converts still in the Sunday-keeping churches? Let's say the World Sunday Law is to become effective soon. Every soul on earth will be forced to worship on Sunday or be killed. So the 144000 are all killed. They are returned to life in glorified bodies, no doubt, because they ascend directly to heaven. "And after these things I saw another angel come down from heaven, having great power; and the earth was lightened with his glory." (Rev. 18:1) Who is this fourth angel? Well who are the three angels of Rev. 14?

Bible Facts About the 144,000

They represent the three messages given by the 144000 during the 1260 days, which is the Loud Cry-Latter Rain period. If you go to Great Controversy p.435, it refers you to the Appendix which explains these three messages as actually one message in three parts comprising a whole. They go together and are not separated by time, or by importance.

People worshipped the sun instead of God since ancient times. Most churches still worship on Sunday, the day named after the sun from the ancient tradition of sun worship. For this reason Babylon has been "fallen" since ancient times. Most of the world has been pagan then Catholic for millenniums, and "fallen." Ever since 1844 the three angels' messages have been calling the world back to the true Creator God who made heaven and earth. Because "Babylon is fallen" this whole system of false worship has been characterized as "the beast" and "If any man worship the beast and his image, the same shall drink of the wine of the wrath of God." The wrath of God is "the seven last plagues; for in them is filled up the wrath of God" (Rev. 15:1)

Since 1844, God has been increasingly saturating the world with more and more truth of the gospel, and of His commandments, and proof of his creatorship. Great strides in science, and astronomy, and medicine prove a Creator. Especially DNA! Heart monitors print out, and prove, that the human heart beats slower on God's Holy Sabbath, no matter whether you are Christian or atheist! See p. 107 of "The Divine Prescription" by Gunther B. Paulien. God created science, and science doesn't lie. As mentioned above, the world has also been steeped in false worship for millenniums. But the day the beast receives total power over "all kindreds, and tongues, and nations" (Rev. 13:7,) that day "I will pour out of my Spirit upon all flesh: and your sons and your daughters shall prophesy, and your young men shall see visions, and your old men shall dream dreams: ... And it shall come to pass, that whosoever shall call on the name of the Lord shall be saved." (Acts 2:17,21) How? By one of the 144000 sent to

John 10:16 and Rev. 18:4

them by a dream or vision to teach them the truth necessary to salvation.

When Satan's church suddenly gets unlimited power to enforce his worship globally, God pours out His unlimited power upon His purified church (the 144000) and anyone who calls on His name (believes in Him) will be saved. The 144000 will be sent by visions and dreams to every believer in Satan's church, who calls for help to escape. Thus the 144000 fulfill the role of the "angel come down from heaven, having great power; and the earth was lightened with his glory." (Rev. 18:1) These glorified 144000 now repeat again that "Babylon the great is fallen" and also bid their new converts to "Come out of her, my people, that ye be not partakers of her sins, and that ye receive not of her plagues." (vs.4) About as soon as the 144000 ascend to heaven, they are immediately sent back to earth again to call their new converts out of the Sunday keeping churches. The timing is so vital that they escape death by not worshipping the beast, and also the plagues by not remaining in a false church.

As soon as the new converts are saved miraculously by the blinding radiance of the 144000 glorified saints seen visibly all over the world, the ten horn power of Rev. 17:16 suddenly realize that they were conned into killing all of God's saints, and they "shall hate the whore, and shall make her desolate and naked, and shall eat her flesh, and burn her with fire." Thus the ten horn power annihilates the beast, which is the first plague. "And the first went and poured out his vial upon the earth; and there fell a noisome and grievous sore upon the men which had the mark of the beast, and upon them which worshipped his image." (Rev.16:2)

Suddenly the new converts are free of the demand to worship a man (the beast is gone) and they begin the long wait for Jesus to return. They had not sacrificed their homes and possessions to the work, as the 144000 had done, but have only to maintain their faith in God throughout the plagues. The 91st Psalm is their experience during the plagues. Read it and see. For the last 45 days they also experience the "time of Jacob's trouble" as their final test of faith.

Before leaving this part let's notice the timing of the fourth angel's message of Rev. 18:1–4 "Come out of her, MY PEOPLE." We must assume they became God's people while still members of the Sunday-keeping churches, for certainly they would not have any inclination to join such a church after they had been converted by the everlasting gospel of the three angels' messages. Leaving these churches too early they would have been killed, and a bit too late, they would "receive of her plagues" as it says. Only the 144000 know exactly who these new converts are. All others, even relatives, are actual enemies, and would gladly betray them. So the 144000 must return immediately from heaven to call them out at exactly the right moment to avoid both death and the plagues. Their worst enemies are destroyed in the first plague, and they are providentially protected throughout the rest of the plagues. (See Ps. 91) The 144000 give the three angels' messages to convert them, and the fourth angel's message to save them from physical harm. Thus the 144000 give all four angels' messages.

Most SDA's have a problem with GC649. They try to show that the 144000 also go through the plagues and go to heaven "without seeing death." They misunderstand the special work and timing of last events, and also wrest Scripture in the process. "These are they which follow the Lamb whithersoever he goeth." These having been translated from the earth, from among the living, are counted as "the firstfruits unto God and to the Lamb." She quoted both from Rev.14:4. Then she quotes from Rev. 7:14, saying, "These are they which came out of great tribulation; they have passed through the time of trouble such as never was since there was a nation." Both of these references are footnoted correctly in the book, thus the reader's fault in reading it, not the author's fault in writing it. But let's take a closer look at it.

John 10:16 and Rev. 18:4

Notice she mentions the 144000 are "translated from among the living." This would be impossible at His Second Coming, because nobody is left alive to watch anybody go up. The wicked are all "slain by the brightness of his coming" (IIThess. 2:8) and the righteous are all taken up "with" the living, not "from" the living. As pointed out earlier, "their enemies beheld them" (Rev. 11:12) as they ascended, and this would account for their translation "from among the living." The living in this case would be the undertakers, because they come alive right in their hands.

Generally I don't take liberties of my own volition, but let me run something by you based on what we have learned so far, and see what you think. You may agree that God is reaching the whole world with the true Bible gospel, with avenues such as 3ABN television, Adventist World Radio, Bible study courses, and in many other ways. It's a continuous process of seed sowing and growth. But when the enemy suddenly is given total power over all people world wide, all these things will be prohibited. God is not willing that a single person be lost who really wants to know God's salvation. Therefore, He takes the work directly into His own hands. He has raised up 144000 who will "follow the Lamb whithersoever He goeth" and "they loved not their lives unto the death." By visions and dreams He sends them secretly "clothed in sackcloth" to "whosoever shall call upon the name of the Lord" to teach them all they need to know to be saved, and calls them out of the Sunday-keeping churches as explained above. They are able to make war with the beast. They will have 1260 literal days for this work, and to prophesy the end. If each of the 144000 gain 100 each, during these 3 1/2 years, it would be 14,400,000! Adding two zeros to 144000 makes 14,400,000 new converts snatched out of the mouth of the dragon, so to speak. They may gain many more each. Right out of Satan's own churches! No wonder Rev. 12:17 says: "And the dragon was wroth with the woman, and went to make war with the remnant of her seed, which keep the commandments of God, and have the testimony of Jesus Christ."

Bible Facts About the 144,000

These new converts are the "great multitude" who live through the "time of trouble, such as never was since there was a nation even to that same time." (Dan. 12:1) These are the ones who wait to greet Jesus when He comes, and are translated "without seeing death." This means there would be a nearly even trade off of neither hot nor cold Laodiceans, replaced by these new converts who are called out of the Sunday keeping churches at Rev. 18:4.

I feel free and safe in the above paragraph because of this quote from Testimonies to Ministers page 300 which says, "Let me tell you that the Lord will work in this last work in a manner very much out of the common order of things, and in a way that will be contrary to any human planning. There will be those among us who will always want to control the work of God, to dictate even what movements shall be made when the work goes forward under the direction of the angel WHO JOINS THE THIRD ANGEL in the message to be given to the world. God will use ways and means by which it will be seen that He is taking the reins into His own hands."

So what is this angel that joins the third angel just before the end, that is so contrary to the third angel? It is Rev. 14:13, the very next verse after the three angels' messages, and after the 144000 are identified once more. The messages from vss.6 to11 are given to the world, but verse 12 and 13 is for the 144000 themselves: "Blessed are the dead which die in the Lord from henceforth." We have already seen that they die at Rev. 11:7, return to life at vs. 11, and ascend to heaven in vs. 12, so that is the blessing. The greatest blessing possible. They are "the firstfruits unto God and to the Lamb."

SIGN OF JONAH

In Matt. 12:38 the scribes and Pharisees asked Jesus for a sign. They had already shut their eyes to some very strong proof that He was the Messiah. He told them, "An evil and adulterous generation seeketh after a sign; and no sign shall be given it, but the sign of the prophet Jonas: For as Jonas was three days and three nights in the whale's belly; so shall the Son of man be three days and three nights in the heart of the earth." (Matt. 12:39–40)

Jesus was only two nights and one day in the tomb, so this saying was never fulfilled to the letter. However, the Bible teaches that the church is also the body of Christ. "For as the body is one, and hath many members, and all the members of that one body, being many, are one body; so also is Christ." (I Cor. 12:12) "Now ye are the body of Christ, and members in particular." vs.27. So when all the saints are killed, (His whole body) as we read in Rev. 11:7, and lay dead for 3 1/2 days (at least a full 72 hours,) vs.9, and return to life again, vs. 11, this saying is fulfilled perfectly, and the "body" is the 144000.

It should be noted that Matt 12:40 is the only time Jesus ever puts it specifically as "three days and three nights," and even likens it to the three days and three nights Jonah was in the whale's belly. Nobody ever considers Jonah's three days and three nights as anything less than a full 72 hours, so we should take Jesus' word as both literal and dual pertaining to the "body" being the 144000.

"As the preaching of Jonah was a sign to the Ninevites, so Christ's preaching was a sign to His generation." (DA 406) Thus Jonah was a symbol of Christ. He prefigured Christ. "In the time of its temporal prosperity Ninevah was a center of crime and wickedness. Inspiration has characterized it as "the bloody city ... full of lies and robbery ... Yet Ninevah, wicked as it had become, was not wholly given over to evil." (PK 265) God sent Jonah to preach repentance, and the people repented. The 144000, will be sent to "whosoever shall call on the name of the Lord to be saved," (Acts 2:21) during the 1260 days of the Latter Rain. These non-Adventists from the Sundaykeeping churches, who repent and forsake their sins by faith in Jesus, will not be trained like the 144000, but will be saved like the thief on the cross. When Peter walked on the water, Jesus merely put out His hand to save him the moment he asked. Likewise the 144000 will rescue anyone who prays to God to escape Satan's kingdom. A doctor may train for ten years, then he can save a life in a moment. The 144000 train for years to "reflect the image of Jesus fully," then, like Jesus, they save souls out of the dragon's mouth, so to speak, in a moment. Same thing. No wonder "the dragon was wroth with the woman, and went to make war with them." Then these new converts will see the dead bodies of the 144000, who were soon raised up in glorified bodies and ascended. Shortly they were sent down again to rescue their new converts from sure death; or as we read EW 278–279, "Servants of God, (144000) endowed with power from on high, with their faces lighted up, and shining with holy consecration, (i.e. in glorified bodies) went forth to proclaim the message from heaven. Souls that were scattered all through the religious bodies answered the call, and the precious (new converts) were hurried out of the doomed churches, as Lot was hurried out of Sodom before her destruction. God's people (the new converts) were strengthened by the excellent glory which rested upon them (the 144000) in rich abundance and prepared them (the new converts) to endure the hour of temptation." For the first plague was due to destroy the doomed churches, and they would have to wait out all the plagues for 1335 days for Christ to return.

THE SEALING TIME

"And after these things I saw four angels standing on the four corners of the earth, holding the four winds of the earth, that the wind should not blow on the earth, nor on the sea, nor on any tree. And I saw another angel ascending from the east, having the seal of the living God and he cried with a loud voice to the four angels to whom it was given to hurt the earth and the sea, Saying, Hurt not the earth, neither the sea, nor the trees, till we have sealed the servants of our God in their foreheads." (Rev. 7:1–3)

These four angels are clearly identified. They are four of the seven angels "to whom it was given to hurt the earth and the sea." vs.2. The only angels that are ever told to hurt the earth and sea are the ones who pour out the seven last plagues. And these four angels are to hold up only "until we have sealed the servants of our God in their foreheads." (vs.3)

The seal of God is the true Sabbath. It's the sign of God's rulership, and His Christian soldiers will die for it. The Sabbath/Sunday question is the deciding factor at the close of probation. Everyone has to choose between the seal of God, and the mark of the beast, to prove which side they are on, as in any war. Then the plagues are poured out on the wicked. "Do it unto others before they do it unto you," is just opposite of, "Do unto others as you would they do to you," Sin is self destructive, so Satan's people turn on each other in a panic, as it was with Gideon's battle. "The Lord set every man's sword against his fellow" to destroy the Midianites. (Judges 7:22)

But why are only four of the seven destroying angels mentioned? Because these are the only four, of the seven, who actually "hurt" the earth, even during the plagues! One angel causes darkness, but darkness doesn't "hurt." It gets dark every night. Another dries up the great river

Euphrates. Whether this is a literal or spiritual drying up doesn't matter in this case because either way, it does no harm to the earth. And one pours out his vial on the sun.

The four destroying angels who do hurt are the first, second, third, and seventh, who pour their vials on the land, the sea, the drinking waters, and the air respectively. And if "to hurt" means destruction, then to "hurt not" has to be just the opposite. If no act of preservation were intended here, but merely a withholding of the plagues, then the command is pointless, because they don't pour until they are told to in Rev. 16:1 anyways.

Obviously this work of preservation is not in the hands of real angels, but only a symbol of human endeavor, as are the three angels' messages a symbol of human endeavor. For instance, these four angels do not control hurricanes, tornadoes, earthquakes, volcanoes, floods, fires by lightening, drought, gypsy moths, locusts, or pestilences. Every one of these kinds of destruction are much worse than any human causes, except possibly a world war. Instead, it represents a human work of preservation, thus we see billions of dollars spent to control oil spills, air pollution, noise of airports and highways, erosion, etc,. None of which has anything to do with the plan of salvation except that when we see these things we know we are in the sealing time which ends with the plagues as the angels let go of the four winds.

"The sealing time is very short, and will soon be over. Now is the time, while the four angels are holding the four winds, to make our calling and election sure." (EW 58) Nobody is actually sealed until he or she voluntarily chooses the seal of God or the mark of the beast, at the last day of probation. But the sealing time parallels the anti-pollution laws several years before. We might liken it to a final exam that takes all day, but a simple check of your score on the way out the door determines your destiny, after which you have no more time to correct anything. Those who believe the exact time, and have gotten the victory over every besetment during the sealing time,

The Sealing Time

will have the faith to choose the seal of God at the last day. The rest are found wanting. They go out to buy more oil, so to speak, but are too late.

After almost two pages talking about the four angels of Rev. 7: 1–3, and still commenting on this text, Ellen White says, "This sealing of the servants of God is the same that was shown to Ezekiel in vision." (TM 445) So let's study the sealing time from Ezekiel 9, since it involves the same group of people and the same time period.

"And he called to the man clothed with linen, which had the writer's inkhorn by his side: And the Lord said unto him, Go through the midst of Jerusalem, and set a mark upon the foreheads of the men that sigh and that cry for all the abominations that be done in the midst thereof. And to the others he said in mine hearing, Go ye after him through the city, and smite: let not your eye spare, neither have ye pity: Slay utterly old and young, both maids, and little children, and women: but come not near any man upon whom is the mark; and begin at my sanctuary. Then they began at the ancient men which were before the house. And he said unto them, Defile the house, and fill the courts with the slain: go ye forth. And they went forth, and slew the city. And it came to pass, while they were slaying them, and I was left, that I fell upon my face, and cried, and said, Ah Lord God! wilt thou destroy all the residue of Israel in thy pouring out of thy fury upon Jerusalem? Then said he unto me, the iniquity of the house of Israel and Judah is exceeding great, and the land is full of blood, and the city full of perverseness: for they say, the Lord hath forsaken the earth, and the Lord seeth not. And as for me also, mine eye shall not spare, neither will I have pity, but I will recompense their way upon their head. And behold, the man clothed with linen, which had the inkhorn by his side, reported the matter, saying, I have done as thou hast commanded me." Ez. 9:3–11

Ellen White says this vision corresponds to the sealing time of Rev. 7: 1–3. Yet this seems like an inverted view of it, like the negative of a snapshot. In Rev. 11 the saints are positively identified and slain to literally defile the earth. Thus Satan tries to purge his camp. But in Ezekiel's vision the saints are likewise marked, but spared, while the wicked are all slain (spiritually) and left to defile the courts (churches.) Thus God purges His Church.

Earlier we likened the sealing time to a final exam, which it really is. And in this exam those who are "taught of God" are filled with His Spirit. They are strengthened to pass the test at the door. They have spiritual life (oil in their lamps) at the close of probation. Even though physically dead, they are raised to ascend. But the unbelievers in the church are not taught of God. They do pretty much as they please. They resist His Spirit. Perhaps being so insensitive to the Spirit they don't even realize they are grieving Him away, and during the sealing time the Spirit is grieved away, leaving them spiritually dead. They defile the church with the abominations that the believers can only sigh and cry about. Lack of the Holy Spirit is spiritual death. The 144000 are finally disfellowshipped for believing and following the Bible rather than the standard teachings of the church, where they conflict.

The very first time Jesus met with His disciples after He arose "He breathed on them, and saith unto them, 'Receive ye the Holy Ghost: Whosesoever sins ye remit, they are remitted unto them; and whosesoever sins ye retain, they are retained.' (John 20:22–23) God Himself raised up our church and breathed the Holy Spirit on the Spirit of Prophecy writings, which, if followed will open heaven to us. This status will continue until the church disfellowships the 144000, who then receive the Holy Spirit of Acts 2:17. From then on only the 144000 will be authorized to issue valid passports, so to speak, having been judged "faultless before the throne of God" and know the way of salvation. The rest of the church will have taken a wrong turn and no longer able to lead people on the right path to heaven. These foolish virgins do not reflect the image of Jesus fully, nor believe His oath, when and how to meet Him.

WHY EXACTLY 144000

Let's notice the similarities between the plan of salvation and a case in court:

COURT	PLAN OF SALVATION
Law	Ten Commandments
Judge	God
Lawyer	Jesus
Other lawyer	Satan
Prisoner	Us
Time	Judgment hour is come
If guilty	Eternal death
If acquitted	Eternal life

Yet one vital element is missing. Where is the jury? Who ever heard of a fair trial without a jury of ones own colleagues? "Do ye not know that the saints shall judge the world?" (I Cor. 6:2) It's true that God is the judge, but a jury brings the final verdict. Thus if a jury should decide "not guilty" the judge cannot pass sentence, but must free the prisoner, even if he, the judge, believes otherwise. If there is still a question on this, please remember that the saints at this point have the mind of Christ, which is fair and unbiased. They have all been in the same boat, and know what is expected to fulfill the law of love under the circumstances.

The very first action in court is to choose a jury. For this a large group of conscientious prospects is summoned to court. In this case, into church, since it involves the moral law. And from these, the jury is carefully selected. Each prospect is meticulously examined by the two lawyers, under the watchful eye of the judge until they

Bible Facts About the 144,000

are satisfied that an unbiased jury of 12 has been chosen for duty. This work has been in progress since 1844. It is called "the investigative judgment." It has taken so long already that many worthy jurors have died of old age and their ranks filled by others. A jury of 12 could not handle the work load, so God has determined to wait until 12000 juries of 12 have reached perfection and to qualify. Thus the 144000 will be taken to heaven for jury duty, having been proved "faultless before the throne of God."

When I was a kid, my brother and I learned to make rhubarb up-side-down cake so as to have it more often. When we would get one done he would say, "Now you cut it and I'll take the first piece." Fair enough, so I would use extra care lest he get an advantage.

Likewise Jesus prepares us for judgment then lets Satan try us, even to death, to make sure. "And they overcame him by the blood of the Lamb, and by ... their testimony and they loved not their lives unto the death." (Rev. 12:11) Those who are thus proven, are resurrected for jury duty in heaven. Even Satan must agree to their innocence; a perfect jury. And now there can be no delay. The last movements will be very rapid. 144000 saints will make up 12000 juries to go over the names of every person who ever claimed to serve God so Christ can reward all the righteous, both living and dead, when He comes 1335 days later. The cases of the wicked are reviewed during the millennium.

In the parable of Matt. 22:1–14, nobody would come to the great wedding feast; they all made excuses. Finally the call was made to the baser classes "and gathered together all as many as they found, both good and bad: and the wedding was furnished with guests. And when the king came in to see the guests, he saw there a man which had not on a wedding garment." "For many are called, but few are chosen" for jury duty.

There are always 12 jurors. God has planned for these juries from way back. "And Jacob called unto his sons, and said, Gather yourselves together, that I may tell you that which shall befall you IN THE LAST DAYS." (Gen.49:1)

Why Exactly 144000

"And I heard the number of them that were sealed: and there were sealed 144000 of all the tribes of THE CHILDREN OF ISRAEL." (Rev. 7:4)

When Jacob told them what was to befall them in the last days, he must have meant their children, for his own sons would not live that long. Nor even their blood relatives which would have limited salvation to the Jews alone. So he must have meant their spiritual progeny (believers) and we, who are spiritual, claim the same Father with them, honor the same government as they, and are loyal to the same eternal law as they were. Thus we are the remnant of their nation if faithful to the call.

"When the books of Daniel and Revelation are better understood, believers will have an entirely different religious experience. They will be given such glimpses of the open gates of heaven that heart and mind will be impressed with the character that all must develop in order to realize the blessedness which is to be the reward of the pure in heart." (TM 114) Thus Ellen White knew there would be much more light to be found in the Bible.

"The judgment is now passing in the sanctuary above. For many years this work has been in progress. Soon, none know how soon, it will pass to the living." (GC 490) Yet there is nothing secret about this if you think it through. "For if we would judge ourselves, we should not be judged." (I Cor.11:13) Does this mean we could escape the judgment? No. It means we can escape the penalty of the judgment. And if we escape the penalty of the judgment, the judgment doesn't affect us; we live on. But how can we judge ourselves? Obviously, by doing right as taught by the Bible, to which we will be compared in the judgment. "Let no man deceive you: he that doeth righteousness is righteous." (I John 3:7)

To make it simple, the judgment began in 1844 when God began to call out a people who recognized the moral law was still binding upon all mankind. When this phase of the judgment is finished, He will have 144000 loyal to the law in every respect, who have judged themselves, so to speak. Suddenly there will be a phase change and judgment "will pass to the living." Every living Adventist who answers the midnight cry, "Behold the bridegroom cometh; go ye out to meet him" will be ready. They leave the company of the foolish virgins (who don't believe it) and thus say: "My Lord delayeth his coming." The "wise" believe and are ready to meet him. The foolish don't believe it and aren't ready to meet Him. Thus judgment passes to the living.

CLOSING PROBATION

The word "probation" is not in the Bible, but what we call the close of probation is clearly indicated in Scripture; one for the church, and one for the world. Probation closes for the church at Matt. 25:10 "and they that were ready went in with him to the marriage (to be His forever) AND THE DOOR WAS SHUT." Those that were shut out tried to get back in but couldn't. Probation for the world closes 1260 days later. "If any man worship the beast, the same shall drink of the wine of the wrath of God." (Rev. 14:9–10) The wrath of God is the seven last plagues (see Rev. 15:1) after probation is closed.

For every event that happens in the end of the world there is a precedent somewhere else in the Bible to guide the saints, for God is the same yesterday, today, and forever. If we know what He did once, we know what He will do again, for "there is no variableness, neither shadow of turning" with Him. (James 1:17)

In Daniel 3 we have a precedent of the close of probation. We all know how the Lord delivered Shadrach, Meshach, and Abednego. King Nebuchadnezzar had commanded all "people, nations, and languages" at the sound of music, to fall down and worship the golden image, which was against God's Law. The king was deliberately trying to set up his word against God's, to prove God either powerless or non-existent. The sound of music was the signal for them to fall down and worship some other god, indicative of the close of probation.

History will be repeated and the beast will demand that all kindreds, tongues, and nations, "and all that dwell upon the earth shall worship him." (Rev. 13:7–8) The day the World Sunday Law becomes effective will be the signal to bow down and worship a man, thus breaking the first and fourth commandments. But the 144000 "loved

Bible Facts About the 144,000

not their lives unto the death" and "the beast that ascendeth out of the bottomless pit shall make war with them, and overcome them, AND KILL THEM." (Rev. 12:11 and 11:7) But as we have already seen they were raised up again 3 1/2 days later and called up to heaven at Rev. 11:11–12. This closes probation and the first plague immediately annihilates the beast power.

Jesus said, "I have yet many things to say unto you, but ye cannot bear them now." (John 16:12) If you read this in context you will see that He was speaking of leaving this world and of His return again later. In the meantime the Spirit of truth would come and "he will guide you into all truth ... and he will shew you things to come." This tells us that we cannot discern truth without the aid of the Spirit. That we cannot understand "things to come" (prophecy) without Him either. Since last day events happen only to the last generation no previous generation need know, nor can they know because they couldn't bear it anyhow He says.

Why couldn't they bear it? A little thought will show why not. For instance can you imagine if Ellen White had explained all these things from Scripture 150 years ago? Not one word of the Bible has changed. Only time has changed, and the work is nearly done. It has been all people could bear just to hear the truth of the Sabbath, the state of the dead, tithing, health reform, and many other things that discourage them from the love of Christ and from sainthood. For one reason or another almost everyone is turned off on some doctrine or another, because they couldn't bear it to be perfect. How many would be able to bear it if the Baptists, and Pentecostals, and the Moral Majority were able to tell people in all honesty that "Adventists preach that all saints must die as martyrs for their faith before Jesus comes, and He is coming soon? We have a better way ... once saved, always saved, and in our church we go directly to heaven when we die, or we go up without dying, or before the great tribulation," etc, etc. So Jesus spared us the real truth of the last days until we would have faith to bear it. If you have been led of the

Spirit to hear Him out this far, maybe He can save you to the uttermost. Let's hope so.

In John 5 Jesus heals the man at the pool of Bethesda, telling him to take up his bed and walk. But it was the Sabbath and the Jews accused Him of breaking the Sabbath. When they learned that He had also healed him on Sabbath they began to "persecute Jesus, and sought to slay him, because he had done these things on the Sabbath day. But Jesus answered them, "My Father worketh hitherto, and I work. Therefore the Jews sought the more to kill him for saying also that God was his Father, making himself equal with God." (John 5:16–18) Then He tells them in no uncertain terms who He really is.

Right after this He miraculously feeds the five thousand and begins to tell them more of His divine mission saying: "I am the bread of life" and "Whoso eateth my flesh, and drinketh my blood, hath eternal life," etc, until they said "This is an hard saying; who can hear it?" Yet He pushed them even further and "From that time many of his disciples went back, and walked no more with him." (John 6:66) He had pushed them to the limit. They couldn't bear it anymore. And for 2000 years He has been pushing us towards perfection to "live by every word that procedeth out of the mouth of God," to eat His flesh and drink His blood. Jesus is the WORD. (See John 1;1) "Thy words were found, and I did eat them." (Jer. 15:16)

One of these days the world will be in such a state that life will be almost intolerable. "And when these things begin to come to pass, then look up, and lift up your heads; for your redemption draweth nigh." (Luke 21:28 and James 5) People tend to think more clearly from a foxhole. When life becomes less secure on earth we think more clearly about heaven and suddenly God is able to reach us with new light that has been right before our eyes all the time.

"These things have I spoken unto you in proverbs; but the time cometh, when I shall no more speak unto you in proverbs, but shall show you plainly of the Father." (John

16:25) In other words before the end it will all be told in such plain language that no one should misunderstand if they really want to know, "None of the wicked shall understand, but the wise shall understand." (Dan. 12:10) Understand what? The exact time; this was the point of the discussion between Christ and Daniel. Last day events make no sense until we are sure of the time based on the most powerful oath in the Bible. Then everything falls into place. All we need to know.

Jesus had to speak to us in proverbs because we couldn't bear it, but the straight testimony of the True Witness will be in plain language when the "time cometh" He says. EW 270 says: "I asked the meaning of the shaking I had seen and was shown that it would be caused by the straight testimony called forth by the counsel of the True Witness to the Laodiceans. This will have its effect upon the heart of the receiver and will lead him to exalt the standard and pour forth the straight truth. Some will not bear this straight testimony. They will rise against it, and this is what will cause a shaking among God's people." The straight truth is all last events, just what you are reading right here based on the oath of Dan.12:7.

Going to the next page, "I asked what had made this great change. An angel answered, 'It is the latter rain, the refreshing from the presence of the Lord, the loud cry of the third angel.'" Now going to the top of EW 86 she says, "At that time the 'latter rain' or the refreshing from the presence of the Lord, will come, to give power to the loud voice of the third angel, and prepare the saints to stand in the period when the seven last plagues shall be poured out." But these saints are non-Adventists. They are all new converts of the 144,000 and are still in the Sunday-keeping churches, for probation had closed for Adventists on the first day of the 1260 days.

Going back a little to why some cannot bear it, let's consider how we talk to small children about Grandma's death, or about where babies come from, etc. Do we tell them plainly as to an adult? At first, Jesus told

His disciples, "Our friend Lazarus sleepeth." But when they wanted to know more about it, He told them plainly, "Lazarus is dead." (John 11:14) And He implied that He let Lazarus die on purpose in order to help their unbelief. (See verse 15)

But there is another reason why "none of the wicked shall understand." It's because they want salvation on their own terms; their mistaken day of worship, state of the dead, the rapture theory, etc. So it's impossible to teach people the facts of last events until they believe the oath of Christ to Daniel, securing the times for all last events. Nothing makes sense to them because nothing fits their fictitious plan of salvation, which they refuse to forfeit for the truth. Only the most unbiased and honest reading can take us to heaven.

If I should say to a small child, "Your Grandmother stopped breathing twenty minutes ago," he might not pick up on it. If I told a doctor, he would know instantly that she was dead. I might convey the same thing by telling him her body is ice cold, or her heart stopped, or her head is gone, etc. Likewise, the Bible doesn't use the word probation, but it describes it in many different ways. The foolish virgins were shut out, the Laodiceans were spewed out, the 144,000 were sealed and the rest were left unsealed, the sheep and goats were separated, and also the wheat from the tares. The more a doctor understands about the basic functions of the body, the more accurately he can pinpoint something wrong with it. And the more we understand the plan of salvation, the more accurately we can pinpoint last events.

So if we believe and understand the dates sworn under oath in Daniel 12 we will believe the events related to them as explained up to this point. One reason we haven't understood it before is because we have made no distinction between the firstfruits (144,000) and the main harvest (great multitude) of Rev. 7.

Let's suppose it's late summer and harvest time draws near. Apples begin to ripen and we give the tree a good shake. Only the first to ripen will fall to the ground. These are called the firstfruits because they are ready first. Also, let's say we are nearing the end of the world and some of the saints have reached perfection (ripened so to speak). The beast demands worship on Sunday but those who are true to God (perfect) would rather die than sin (worship a man). They are ripe and fall to the ground when tested by persecution. But 3 1/2 days later they return to life and ascend. Thus they are the ones who die in the Lord "from henceforth" and are blessed. "Blessed are the dead which die in the Lord from henceforth." (Rev. 14:13) And, as implied, cursed are the living who sin to avoid death from now on. Thus, "The substitution of ... Sunday in place of the Bible Sabbath is the last act in the drama." (7T 141) The beast claims to be God, so he demands worship as God. This is stolen identity, and those who are deceived by this fact lose everything, like a credit card theft.

The Bible confirms all that we have been learning about the death and resurrection of the 144000. TM 300 also says: "Let me tell you that the Lord will work in this last work in a manner very much out of the common order of things, and in a way that will be contrary to any human planning." Why? Because planting and nurturing a crop is a whole different work than mowing it down, or slaughtering it for storage. Which is more important to a farmer, seedtime or harvest? Evangelism (soul winning) must give way to the judgment hour sooner or later. She goes on to say: "There will be those among us who will always want to control the work of God, to dictate even what movements shall be made when the work goes forward under the direction of the angel who joins the third angel in the message to be given to the world." If angels in Rev. 14 represent messages, then what is the message that joins the third angel in this last work? Let's consider this. Growing it then killing it is like seedtime and harvest. In the Bible they are called the Early and Latter Rain, with a specific time for each. Who dare say we are not nearing the harvest? And does the Bible mention this additional message anywhere for sure? Yes it does, right after the

Closing Probation

third angel's message, and thus connected with them. The subject is death. "And I heard a voice from heaven saying unto me, Write, Blessed are the dead which die in the Lord from henceforth: (from now on) Yea, saith the Spirit, that they may rest from their labours; and their works do follow them." (Rev. 14:13) Please notice the promised blessing. When are they blessed? Three and a half days after they die. "And after three days and an half the Spirit of life from God entered into them, and they stood upon their feet; And they heard a great voice saying unto them, Come up hither. And they ascended up to heaven in a cloud." (Rev.11:11-12) Thus they receive the greatest blessing possible to man!

So the rest of Rev. 14 describes the fate of these two classes of people. Rev. 14: 14-16 is the harvest of the firstfruits (144000), and 17-20 is what happens to the wicked during the plagues. Neither of these passages represent the Second Coming of Jesus for in verse 14 "one sat like unto the Son of man" is not actually Him at all, but only like him, it says. A likeness is only a resemblance, not the real thing. If I say, "You look just like you father," it doesn't mean I can't tell the difference, but only that I see a resemblance; a likeness. And when 144000 people suddenly stand up on their feet after being dead for three days, and then float right up to heaven, people who confuse the rapture theory with the Second Coming will be fooled by this resemblance. To them it seems like the end of the world. And immediately after the 144000 ascend, the plagues are poured out on the wicked, which also seems like the end of the world to the misinformed. But Jesus doesn't return before the plagues. This harvest is only the firstfruits of the harvest. I Thess. 4:13-18 is the real return of Jesus, "For the Lord HIMSELF shall descend from heaven," and not merely a resemblance of Him. Rev. 14:14-17 doesn't say one word of His Coming, only that one sat on a cloud, to see if we can be fooled to just take something for granted that it doesn't say at all.

Since you have read to this point you may have wondered who the two witnesses of Rev.11 are. First we must realize that there are various ways to take the word "witness." The Old and New Testaments be called the two witnesses, yet, from cover to cover they are one witness against sin. The Old Testament points forward to Christ; the New Testament back to Christ. The harvest of the earth is also in two parts; the 144000 before the close of probation, with Christ still interceding in the sanctuary, and the great multitude after the close of probation, after He leaves the sanctuary. One proves, or witnesses, that sin can be conquered and perfection reached while we still have an Intercessor, and one to witness that the Law can be kept perfectly without an Intercessor after probation has closed. Thus no one can ever claim he lived in a time that perfection is impossible. The two witnesses prove it both ways, and on a wholesale scale. Jesus was tried more than any of us as a witness against sin. He was without an intercessor during His whole life on earth, and we can do the same by obeying the Holy Spirit as He did.

Believers are born again Christians. "Whosoever is born of God, doth not commit sin; for his seed (Jesus) remaineth in him: and he cannot sin, because he is born of God." (I John 3:9) Can a honey bee eat carrion? No. Why not? Because a honey bee is a whole different creature than a maggot. So let's reverse the text above like this: Whosoever is NOT born of God, cannot keep from sin; for his seed (Satan) remaineth in him: and he cannot keep from sin, because he is NOT born of God. Thus if you don't break the Law, it has no effect on you, not even in the judgment, for Jesus (the seed) remains in full control. Love fulfills the Law. Whose love? Jesus' love. It's a gift. It's a miraculous re-creation. You have a holy heart.

When I pick over beans I judge every bean. Some may be perfect. Some may need a bit of dusting off but are perfect otherwise. Some are hopeless. If all were perfect I needn't even look them over. So the judgment is necessary only because of the wicked. Even the wicked do not all deserve the same punishment, so we have to decide what is fair. "And that servant, which knew his lord's will, and prepared not himself, neither did according to his will, shall be beaten with many stripes. But he that knew not, and did commit things worthy of stripes, shall be beaten with few stripes." (Luke 12:47–48)

As noted at the beginning of these studies we are all in a state of hypnotism. Our subconscious minds are deranged and we are powerless to turn from our natural sinful ways until this spell is broken. Only Scripture applied by the Holy Spirit can break the spell of Satan over us. If we could do it ourselves we would need no Saviour to show us the way. Only by Scripture and the Law can we detect wrongs. When we discover a problem in our lives, we need to "hunger and thirst for righteousness" and tell God we want to be made to hate the things we love that are wrong. To consult our own feelings in the matter is no good because our feelings are biased and will only lead us to destruction. (Prov. 14:12)

LUKE 17:33-37 AND MISCELLANEOUS

"Whosoever shall seek to save his life shall lose it; and whosoever shall lose his life shall preserve it. I tell you, in that night there shall be two men in one bed; the one shall be taken and the other left. Two women shall be grinding together; the one shall be taken and the other left. Two men shall be in the field; the one shall be taken, and the other left. And they answered and said unto him, where, Lord? And he said unto them, wheresoever the body is, thither will the eagles be gathered together." (Luke 17:33-37)

The subject is life or death. An unbiased and strict reading of this passage proves that the righteous are the ones that are "taken," not the wicked. It cannot be taken the wrong way without wrenching Scripture. It must be taken exactly as it reads because it is a literal statement without a single symbol to be changed or guessed at.

For instance let's go over it again taking it just as it reads. Two classes of people are mentioned here. One that seeks to save his life, and one that doesn't. One is taken; the other left. But neither makes this decision, for one of them is taken by force, at the discretion of the executioner. Obviously the executioner arrives with prior knowledge of who is to be "taken," and who is to be "left" undisturbed. No element of doubt is mentioned, because it doesn't exit. Why? Because both parties have already made their free choice to worship the true God on pain of death, or to worship the beast to avoid death temporarily. The executioner has positive identification with no chance of error, because he has been given a list from church records.

Now you may accuse me of "interpreting" and not taking it as it reads after all. No matter who explains this passage must of necessity apply it to the future. The problem is, people have a very wrong notion of last events based on erroneous readings elsewhere, and not on the oath of Christ. Thus they "guess" at what this means rather than what will actually happen according to an honest reading of the whole matter of last events. Nowhere in the Bible are the wicked ever taken bodily, one by one, from the righteous, but just the opposite. The wicked are dealt with en mass in the plagues, or in hell-fire. The wicked always out number the righteous. If a farmer find only ten good plants in a field, he saves them one by one and then plows the whole field. Same thing. So "he shall send his angels with a great sound of a trumpet, and they shall gather together his elect from the four winds, from one end of heaven to the other." (Matt. 24:31) Carefully one by one.

The disciples seemed to know Jesus meant the righteous were the ones "taken," so they asked "Where, Lord?" not "Who, Lord?" Jesus said their bodies would attract the eagles, leaving no doubt where. And He had already said that "whosoever shall lose his life shall preserve it." But the only way to "preserve" life after death is by the resurrection. This also proves the righteous are the ones taken and killed, because in so doing their lives are preserved by resurrection. The wicked are also resurrected, of course, but are not preserved. They are resurrected to be destroyed. Thus this passage is but another account of the death of the 144000.

Jesus has instant and perfect power over death. But this benefits only those who believe and trust Him in death, knowing He can resurrect them. Jesus told His disciples He was glad Lazarus died because it gave Him a chance to help their unbelief. (See John 11:4 and 15) And if He was glad Lazarus died, He will be glad when the 144000 believe and trust Him in death also. Lazarus suffered no harm in death. Neither will the 144000. Death is only a sleep. Death doesn't hurt. Fear of death hurts. Fear is very scary. "Perfect love casteth out fear." (I John 4:18) If we believe Jesus destroyed the works of the devil, why should we fear? And if we have inordinate fear of death, it's because we aren't ready for it. (see Heb. 2:14–14)

Bible Facts About the 144,000

The fear of death is one of Satan's best weapons. Thus our news is full of it. So are our movies, and the operas, and classic literature, and history books. We are brain washed (hypnotized) to fear death, because we are on Satan's ground. But heaven will not be tainted by the fear of death. Meantime, as Christians let's drive carefully, but let's be glad to die for Jesus if He needs us to at any moment, and erase all fictitious notions of death. We need to think of heaven as our home, and to act accordingly.

For years we have been taught (not from the Bible) that the 144000 and the great multitude of Rev.7:9 all go to heaven at the Second Coming. The word (firstfruits) means they reach perfection and maturity before the rest. If not, the word is pointless; even a lie.

Also we have been taught (not from the Bible) that the 144000 can expect to be translated "without seeing death." If the 144000 are translated together with the great multitude, what distinguishes one group from the other? They would have to be all firstfruits, or all main harvest. And if so, who are killed and resurrected to ascend in Rev. 11? We know they are saints because they ascend to heaven. This is the "special resurrection?"

To those who quote Ellen White saying we are not to be "tested" on time again, let's think of it this way. Every kid is "tested" while he learns to use a clock, a calendar, or to make change for a dollar. But after he has thoroughly learned how to do these things it is no longer a test for him. If we know we should do something, but don't do it, it's not a test, it is disobedience, pure and simple. Tests are for teaching purposes. Obedience is for the road.

"The words are closed up and sealed till the time of the end." (Dan. 12:9) So the time is sealed up by time itself until history unfolds almost to the end of the world. This is the first seal. The second seal is prejudice. How is that? Because "none of the wicked shall understand." It doesn't say nobody shall understand, but only the wicked don't understand. For all practical purposes, a person who shuts his eyes can't see a bit better than a truly blind person. Likewise the time can only be known to those who believe and obey. Let's say a man sees a train blocking the road in front of him. He sees it in plenty of time to stop, but he deliberately runs into it. Not because he's blind, but because he didn't want to see it. He sort of wishes it weren't there. The wicked don't want to know the time, and pay no attention to facts, or reason, or common sense. They are beyond help from any direction because it interferes with their own private agenda. "If God gets in my way, I have no choice but to run over Him!" is their attitude. "And this is the condemnation, that light is come into the world and men loved darkness rather than light, because their deeds were evil. For everyone that doeth evil hateth the light, neither cometh to the light, lest his deeds should be reproved. But he that doeth truth cometh to the light, that his deeds may be made manifest that they are wrought in God." (John 3:19–20) "But the path of the just is as a shining light, that shineth more and more unto the perfect day." (Prov. 4:18)

The exact time is of no use to the dead. They simply remain dead and beyond the reach of Satan to molest, come when He may. But the exact time is very vital to the last generation (the living,) and they must know and be ready to meet Him by the precise Bible texts we are discussing here.

Here is Luke 17:33–37 again with comments: "Whosoever shall seek to save his life (by worshipping the beast) shall lose it (in the plagues); and whosoever shall lose his life (to the beast) shall preserve it (by rising 3 1/2 days later). I tell you, in that night (The World Sunday Law will be enacted at midnight) there shall be two men in one bed; (Satan does his work in darkness) the one shall be taken and the other shall be left (selection is perfect, they have the church list.) Two women shall be grinding together; the one shall be taken and the other left (sex is no barrier). Two men shall be in the field; the one shall be taken, and the other left. (Half the earth is dark at the time of the killing. Or, any missed in the dark are killed in broad day light. One way or the other, or both.) "And they answered and said unto him, Where, Lord? And he said unto them, Wheresoever the body is, thither will the eagles be gathered together."

THE KINGDOM OF HEAVEN

"And when he was demanded of the Pharisees when the kingdom of God should come, he answered them and said, The kingdom of God cometh not with observation: Neither shall they say, Lo here! or, lo there! for, behold, the kingdom of God is within you. (Luke 17:20-21) Jesus was not noted for idle words. When Daniel asked Him the same question, He gave him the exact time secured by His most powerful oath. But He answered the Pharisees in a spiritual sense rather than literally, and spiritual matters are discerned only by those who mind the Spirit. Thus "The (spiritual) kingdom of God cometh not with observation (visibly) ... behold, the kingdom of God is within you." Since only the spiritual receive the kingdom "within," only the spiritual are translated to heaven at the last day.

God intended each man and wife and family to be a little heaven on earth. If they are spiritual their love and trust will increase, and any tensions and misunderstandings will decrease until they reflect the image of Jesus fully.

God intended for His church to be a little heaven on earth. You don't have to be perfect to join the church. You join the church to learn perfection. And when you reflect the image of Jesus fully, you are one of God's "Holy People" spoken of in Dan.12:7.

LOVE

"Love is of God, and everyone that loveth is born of God, and knoweth God. He that loveth not, knoweth not God; for God is love." (I John 4:7–8) Who is worthy to add anything to this? The world could not hold all the books that could comment on this. John, who wrote Revelation became speechless and gave up like this: "And there are also many other things which, if they should be written every one, I suppose that even the world itself could not contain the books that should be written. AMEN." This is the very last verse of John's gospel. But I can't resist just one comment on "love:" It's a gift! Don't refuse it. You don't have it by nature until born again.

A NEW HEAVEN AND EARTH

Every single time the Bible mentions recreating a new earth it always says a new "HEAVEN and earth." Why is that? The earth was destroyed by Noah's flood, but what would that have to do with heaven? Certainly nothing happened to the starry heaven anyway. Nor the throne of God. So let's take a look at the BLUE SKY. "And God said, Let there be a firmament in the midst of the waters, and let it divide the waters from the waters. And God made the firmament, and divided the waters which were under the firmament from the waters which were above the firmament: and it was so." (Gen. 1:6–7) "and it was so" means "believe it or not." You'll see.

Verse 20 says the firmament is where the birds fly; the air. Also notice that water is always mentioned in the plural, "waters." So how many kinds of water do we have? Water can be liquid, gas, or solid. But whether it is water, steam, or ice, it's still H_2O unless it be atomized to hydrogen and oxygen.

Apparently the word "firmament" means more that just "air." "Air" is used three times in this same chapter, but not here. And in vs. 16 "God made two great lights" "and God set them in the firmament of the heaven to give light upon the earth." vs. 17 We just read in vs. 6, "let there be a firmament in the midst of the waters." We don't mind the air in the midst of the waters, but to put the sun there too is a little much, don't you think? So obviously the "firmament" can include about anything overhead. We'll work on this a little more. For now let's assume that the process of Noah's flood not only altered the earth drastically, but also heaven, (blue sky) as well, since both are to be recreated again like they were in the beginning. So what actually happened to the sky anyhow? Does the Bible tell us anywhere? I think it does. Let's see what it says:

"In the six hundredth year of Noah's life, in the second month, the seventeenth day of the month, the same day were all the fountains of the great deep broken up, and the windows of heaven were opened. And the rain was upon the earth forty days and forty nights." (Gen. 7:11 and 12) The first thing that happened was this: "ALL the fountains of the great deep were broken up." Whatever this means it must have caused the next thing mentioned: "and the windows of heaven were OPENED," and since whatever these two things mean, they caused it to rain for forty days.

First we ought to figure out how much water came down in those forty days and forty nights. If it rained 3 inches every 8 hours, it would be 9 inches every 24 hours, and 9x40days=360 inches, which is 30 feet of water; total! This is not deep enough to cover a tree! Yet "the waters prevailed exceedingly upon the earth; and all the high hills, that were under the whole heaven, were covered. Fifteen cubits upward did the waters prevail; and the mountains were covered." (vs. 19–20)

We all know that outdoor air weighs 14.7 psi at sea level. A water pump can only draw up about 30 ft of water from a well due to the weight of air above. My point is this: All the air in the world only weighs as much as 30 ft of water, and could under no circumstances hold its own weight of water and turn it into rain! And even if it did, it would only be 30 ft deep, and could never cover all the mountains of the earth! So where did all the extra water come from? We just read it above. It came from "all the fountains of the great deep" that were broken up. Since the flood, about 3/4th the earth is oceans, and they are several miles deep in places. Before the flood most of it was underground, and it circulated in a network of caves and tunnels, heated by volcanic heat for even temperatures from the equator to the poles. Adam and Eve needed no clothing to protect them from the elements. In fact, they are the only animal without natural protection of some kind other than skin.

A New Heaven and Earth

But what about "the windows of heaven" that "were opened?" Maybe the heaven was altered after all. Maybe there was a solid shell of transparent ice around the whole earth held up by air pressure! A hole in a wall could let in light, but it takes a window to keep out the cold as well. Think of the benefits of a shell of ice like a window a few miles up. The sun could shine through. The super cold of outer space could not mix with air to cause rain, snow, jet streams, tornadoes, hurricanes, and polar ice caps, because the whole earth was indoors, so to speak, and the temperature was so mild and even, there could scarcely be a draft anywhere. Remember, God made the world perfect. No thunderbolts to scare them half to death. No earthquakes were possible because the thick ledge under ground was all one solid, unbroken piece until "the great deep was broken up." No volcanoes for the same reason. The ledge held them where God created them. No tornadoes or hurricanes because turbulence cannot occur in all cold air, or all warm air, only in a mixture, which couldn't happen with the ice (windows) all in place, (north south east and west). There was something up there to petition the outer space and cold from mixing. In fact, it couldn't even rain! "But there went up a mist from the earth, and watered the whole face of the ground." (Gen. 2:6) It couldn't rain, because there wasn't enough difference in temperature either in the sky above, or at the poles, to cause it to rain! It could only mist.

Now back to Gen.1:7 where it says the air divided the waters which were under the air (surface water) from the water which was above the air (the shell of ice.) Only airtight ice could stay up there. If any air could get by it, or through it, it would be IN the air, not ABOVE the air. And only ice could stay frozen from the super cold above. We all know that a high mountain near the equator stays perpetually ice capped while the base of it is tropical heat.

Adam and Eve had all the air that we have today, plus the 30 ft of ice, making double air pressure on them. This gave them much more energy than we have. It was just the opposite of climbing a mountain into thin air, which makes us tire easily, and affects our metabolism; mountain sickness. It acted like a supercharger on a race car, giving them much greater energy than we have.

Adam and Eve were created to live forever. They never got tired. They never had to sleep. All these benefits will be back when the earth is made new again. There was no night there either. Can you imagine sitting around in the dark all night, every night, for the sun to come up? For them it should have been half of forever.

"And God made two great lights; the greater light to rule the day, and the lesser light to rule the night: he made the stars also." (Gen.1:16) We take it for granted this means the sun and the moon, and we never give it a second thought. But neither sun nor moon are mentioned here; only lights. But the moon makes no light; it all comes from the sun. Besides that, it's on the wrong side half the time anyways. Even in a full moon you can't read by moonlight, even with a magnifying glass. But have you ever heard of fiber optic light? God made the shell of ice transmit light all four ways around the earth (sidewise) so there never was any night there until the heat rose up from all that warm water that broke out of bounds and melted the ice in forty days. The thirty ninth day it still acted as a window, but the fortieth day it was gone.

"Hast thou with him spread out the sky, which is strong, and as a molten looking glass." (Job 37:18) Thirty feet of solid ice 5 or 10 miles in the sky could be fairly strong, but not now. It's not strong enough to even bump your head on. To say it looks as shiny as a looking glass would be a very good description of it, also. They say Job was about the earliest Bible writer. He may have seen it.

"Out of whose womb came the ice? and the hoary frost of heaven, who gendered it? The waters are hid as with a stone, and the face of the deep is frozen." (Job 38;29–30) A womb indicates a very special creation; a miracle. Here he speaks of the frost of heaven, even calling it ice,

A New Heaven and Earth

and water as solid as a stone. The very next verses tell of Arcturus, and Pleiades, and Mazzaroth, and Orion, all proven true by modern science. Why should we doubt his knowledge of the shell of ice only five or ten miles above when he was so accurate about these mighty stars, many light years away?

At Noah's flood the shell of ice melted away and the surface of the earth was left mostly water, leaving the earth badly messed up, and a lot of it was totally uninhabitable. Next time it will be destroyed by fire. All the air and water will "pass away with a great noise!" No plumber can solder a pipe with water in it. So it seems reasonable that the elements will not melt while covered with oceans of water either. They pass away with a great noise, THEN "the elements melt with fervent heat." "Nevertheless we, according to his promise, look for new heavens and a new earth, wherein dwelleth righteousness." (2 Peter 3: 13)

To sum up, let's take a look at the wreckage. Detectives can build a pretty good case just from the wreckage after a big jumbo jet crashes and kills everybody in it. Likewise when the great deep was broken up it left huge ledges tilting up at all angels that we still see along the superhighways. Also many of the great networks of underground tunnels and deep caves and caverns remain, much as they were created to circulate warm water all around the earth. Some still carry water underground for long distances even today. In many parts of the world, they still produce warm water. Some even produce boiling water and live steam and geysers. But these are probably due to disruption rather than original design. A geyser squirting boiling water up a hundred feet was too dangerous and scary for a perfectly safe world. Earthquakes were impossible when the earth was all one unbroken piece of thick ledge, but ever since the flood, these pieces have been grinding and slipping with violent consequences. Since the flood, 3/4th of the earth is uninhabitable oceans. Great deserts, great rain forests, great mountainous regions and bad lands may be considered natural wonders for dare devils, but very uncomfortable habitat. So are the great polar regions, which used to be paradise just like the rest of the world. In many parts of today's world, the weather runs to extremes from no rain at all, to a constant down pour for weeks or months. Large areas are at risk of deadly tornadoes, hurricanes, forest fires, and earthquakes. Natural disasters are on the increase.

And before all this wreckage, the earth produced all manner of fruit for food at arm's reach. The whole earth was all the same mild temperature, and produce grew of its own accord everywhere, year round. God furnished everything for free. No work. No Pain.

MONEY PART I

"The love of money is the root of all evil" they say, but in the new world there will be no need of money. In this world most things are supplied by human effort. Human effort (labor) means work, and where work and pain are practically synonymous, it boils down to trading comfort for pain, (money for work) or pain for comfort (work for money.) Pain was unknown until sin entered the picture, because God supplied every need for life, no work was necessary to live. When Adam sinned he took over his own livelihood, and God said "cursed is the ground for thy sake; in sorrow shalt thou eat of it all the days of thy life" (Gen.3:17) and work and pain entered. When sin is eradicated, and our needs are supplied by God again, there will "be no more death, neither sorrow, nor crying, neither shall there be any more pain; for the former things are passed away." (Rev. 21:4) Money in this world is only a means of measuring pain. The harder the work, the more it costs. The law, and the police make sure we play fair, and don't take out more than we kick into the economy. We have to play fair with ourselves just as we should have been fair with God. When we learn to love one another, and to love God again, we will be returned to the original plan, and we will not need money, because we won't have to work.

When gold was used for trade it had its own intrinsic value. But an ounce of gold may be worth a ton of paper, so gold money is weighed out to determine its value, while paper money is determined by the amount written on the face of it, and accepted at face value. It is worthless of itself, and only accepted on faith, like a personal check, or an oral promise. The only difference between any of these is a matter of integrity. So far the government hasn't failed, but it is riskier than gold. A personal check is more apt to fail than a federal note. An oral promise is secure as long as the friendship lasts. Since nothing is secured by gold or silver, all business is done on faith except where a legal title is retained until an item is fully paid for. You know all this.

But at original creation, God supplied all the necessities of life; all food grew automatically and free for the picking. No clothing nor housing was needed, because there was mild, warm air from pole to pole. No schools were needed because a kid was educated only once, and forever, by watching others; and since there was no sin, no one would have been misinformed about anything. No wars, no armies, no schools, no hospitals, no roads, nor anything requiring taxes, pain, or compulsion. Taxes are necessary to replace God. When God supplied all our needs, nobody had to be taxed to build pyramids, hanging gardens, and to fight wars ad infinitum, to the pride, vanity and greed of cruel kings, dictators, and popes.

Our economy is really all one ball of wax, so to speak. We are all bound together in a community effort. Nobody makes a pair of shoes any more. Even in the shoe factory nobody makes a pair of shoes. The factory makes the shoes, and each worker adds some tiny bit to a hundred pairs a day. He can do the same thing to a lot of shoes, faster than he can do a lot of things to one shoe. This speeds up the work, and cuts down the cost. This same team work is applied to practically everything under the sun, and the easier the work, the lower the cost of living. This is all well and good, providing nothing disrupts the process.

But the more we specialize, the more interdependent we become, and the more disastrous if anything disrupts the process. Something go wrong, and everything comes crashing down. For instance, the money could fail again, as it did in the Great Depression. Only it would be far worse because everything is more specialized now, and more dependent on team work. In the early thirties, millions still had their own gardens, small farms, and horses. Today a relatively few people run mammoth tractors and highly

Money Part I

specialized food production, which is very vulnerable to cash flow, to oil, and electricity. Trouble could bring everything to a stand still. And for the same reason, practically everything else would fail also. Like a row of dominos. Or let's say sun storms should fry our satellites, and our communication systems should fail? Or the stock market? Or a wholesale power failure? We would be worse off than the birds and animals who still depend entirely on God for their food which grows of itself. They have natural protection from the weather. They pay no taxes, don't smoke, drink, or do drugs. They discipline their own young, like a mother bear. The point is, the more team work, the higher the production, the lower the costs, but it's like climbing a ladder, or building higher and higher, ad infinitum, until an inevitable crash due to sin and misunderstanding among us. Common sense tells us that disaster could strike any moment in such a highly specialized economy without perfect love and trust. Our money is only paper. Nobody makes their own electricity. If it failed in the winter, oil heat would fail, pipes would freeze. All food is trucked into the cities. No money, no fuel to truck food, and no fuel to farm it.

The crash is inevitable, and millions will starve in the cities. Even the undertakers will be starved, and to prevent spreading disease from the millions of unburied dead, anyone trying to get in or out will be shot on the spot.

Not one of the 144000 will be caught in a city, because they are watching, and will obey the warning to get out of the cities. "In the day when the Son of man is revealed, in that day…he which shall be upon the housetop, and his stuff in the house, let him not come down and take it away:" (Luke 17:30–31) Look up the word "cities" in the E.G.W. indexes. After you read this book, you may have a little time to take heed, and to warn others to get out in time.

Ideally, a Christian family is a closed loop system. They don't punch a time clock for pay; each does his or her own part based on love, not money. When one is happy, they are all happy. When one is hurt, they all hurt. They all agree to rules that aren't even written down. They all know what each other likes and doesn't like. Same in heaven. There will be no unfair government in heaven. In fact all will be completely self-governed, and no need of coercive government. "For if we would judge ourselves, we should not be judged." (I Cor.11:32) We will love God, and each other impartially. If we do no one any wrong, we need no correction. If there be any chance we might not be safe to take to heaven, God will know, and we just won't be there. "Be ye therefore perfect even as your father in heaven is perfect."(Matt. 5:48) It's the perfect solution in last events. Only God can make us perfect, but only if we ask Him.

MONEY PART 2

"Go to now, ye rich men, weep and howl for your miseries that shall come upon you. Your riches are corrupted, and your garments are moth eaten. Your gold and silver is cankered; and the rust of them shall be a witness against you, and shall eat your flesh as it were fire. Ye have heaped treasure together for the last days." (James 5:1–3)

People who see this manuscript may think I am time-setting the end of the world. But all I do is try to call your attention to the time God has set in Dan 12 and hope the Holy Spirit will convince you.

Nevertheless, now I want to call your attention to current news from our local newspaper that should give you a clue to how soon God may reveal to us the exact day of probation and the end of the world in the near future.

For your information I will give some real calendar dates to put it in perspective. Quoting from U S News & World Report 10/25/04: "The United States has now reached its legal borrowing ceiling of $7.384 trillion." Then on 11/19/04, the Bangor Daily News said: "With the government facing imminent default because it has depleted its authority to borrow money, the debt limit bill would pump up its borrowing cap to $8.18 trillion. That is 70 percent the size of the entire U.S. economy, and more than $2.4 trillion higher than the debt Bush inherited upon taking office in 2001."

This means that, with the extra expenses of catastrophic natural disasters, and still warring in Iraq, our country could be bankrupt before Bush leaves office. Ouch! What does this mean? It means your home, business, town, state and the whole country will be taken over by the loan sharks who purposely fomented wars to loan us money and to systematically bankrupt us. "for thy merchants were the great men of earth; for by thy sorceries were all nations deceived." (Rev.18:23) The same super rich men that James named above.

No shots need be fired, but a confederacy of "ten horns. ... which are ten kings, which have received no kingdom as yet; but receive power as kings (United Nations maybe?) one hour with the beast ... .shall give their power and strength unto the beast." (Rev.17:12–13) In the next verse they make war with the Lamb, and His army of 144000 as explained throughout this study.

Some, no doubt, will wait until the country actually goes bankrupt before they will consider it time to start "trimming their lamps," since it is considered heresy to know the time. After bankruptcy the ten horns begin to negotiate getting the power to transfer it to the beast. Nobody knows how long it will take, but probably not too long, but even the most nominal Adventists should realize that the day the beast is given power will be the day we can start counting the 2595 days to the return of Jesus. The days left from now through the bankruptcy, and through the transfer of power to the beast will be like the summer of 1844, just before the October 22 day ending the 2300 days of Dan. 8:14. Let's review what those days were like, because history will be repeated.

The whole purpose of these studies is to help us understand present truth, and to be ready for eternity. I don't want to mislead or let you down. I've been watching and merely try to give you what I have discovered, so you can decide what to do for yourself. In 1844 God ran a firedrill, so to speak, so we could benefit by their experience, only this time it's the real thing. So let me quote some of the feelings and experiences from that time.

In October 1844 Ellen White was 16 years old. She turned 17 on November 26, and had her first vision sometime in the next month. She had attended William Miller's first lectures in Portland in March 1840 when she was 12 years old. June 26, 1842 she was baptized

Money Part 2

into the Casco Street Methodist Church. Also about this time Miller was back in Portland for his second series of meetings. The Millerites had not determined the correct day to end the 2300days of Dan. 8:14 yet. They had first expected it to end in 1843. Then they thought it would be on April 21, 1844.

Here are excerpts from Vol. I of Arthur White's life of E.G.W. p. 46: "Advent believers were now living in the terminal year of the 2300-year prophecy of Daniel 8:14, the year of the expected Advent. This, according to the accepted form of Jewish reckoning, would terminate on April 21, 1844." In simple language Ellen has given an account of what took place:

"Unity and peace now dwelt among our people who were looking forward to the coming of the Lord. How carefully and tremblingly did we approach the time of expectation. We sought, as a people, with solemn earnestness to purify our lives that we might be ready to meet the Saviour at His coming. Notwithstanding the opposition of ministers and churches, Beethoven Hall, in the city of Portland, was nightly crowded, and especially was there a large congregation on Sundays ... .

"Meetings were still held at private houses in different parts of the city with the best results. Believers were encouraged to work for their friends and relatives, and conversions were multiplying day by day. " (I Life Sketches p. 180.)

She "recalled that the rich and the poor, the high and the low, ministers and laymen, crowded into Beethoven Hall to hear the doctrine of the Second Advent. At each meeting a short, pointed discourse was given, and the way was opened for general exhortation. The spirit of opposition was held in check.

"The presence of holy angels was felt," and she added, "The numbers were being added to the little band of believers." (ILS p. 181) During the last weeks leading up to April 21, 1844 preparation for the event became paramount.

101

She reports: "Worldly business was for the most part laid aside for a few weeks. We carefully scrutinized every thought and emotion of our hearts as if upon our death-beds and in a few hours to close our eyes forever upon earthly scenes. There was no making "ascension robes" for the great event; we felt the need of internal evidence that we were prepared to meet Christ, and our white robes were purity of soul, character cleansed from sin by the atoning blood of our Saviour. But the time of expectation passed. This was the first close test brought to bear upon those who believed and hoped that Jesus would come in the clouds of heaven.

"The disappointment of God's waiting people was great. The scoffers were triumphant and won the weak and cowardly to their ranks. Some who had appeared to possess true faith seemed to have been influenced only by fear, and now their courage returned with the passing of the time, and they boldly united with the scoffers declaring they had never been duped to really believe the doctrine of Miller, who was a mad fanatic. Others, naturally yielding or vacillating, quietly deserted the cause." (p. 184,185)

What they felt and thought in anticipation of the Second Coming more than 160 years ago, mostly in New England, will be repeated on a much grander scale worldwide this time. As the day of expectation approached, "Every moment seemed precious and of the utmost importance to me. I felt that we were doing work for eternity, and that the careless and uninterested were in the greatest peril. My faith was unclouded, and I appropriated the precious promises of Jesus to myself ... .

"With diligent searching of hearts and humble confession we came prayerfully up to the time of expectation. Every morning we felt it was our first business to secure the evidence that our lives were right before God. We realized that if we were not advancing in holiness we were sure to retrograde. Our interest for each other increased; we prayed much with and for each other.

"We assembled in the orchards and groves to commune with God and to offer our petitions to Him, feeling more clearly His presence when surrounded by His natural works. The joys of salvation were more necessary to us than our food and drink. If clouds obscured our minds we dared not rest or sleep till they were swept away by consciousness of our acceptance with the Lord." (p. 188, 189)

This is the way every Christian should live day by day, but especially so as we near the end of this world's history. The sooner, and the more diligently we practice this from now on the better. We mustn't be careless with all eternity a stake. Nothing could possibly be more important than this. I saw a church sign once that said: "We only live once, but if we do it right, it's enough."

It never ceases to amaze me that my Adventist friends say we are never to know the time, because it would be a deterrent to being ready. But clearly the experiences of the people just before the time in 1844 prompted them to put forth an effort toward repentance they never could have reached otherwise in getting ready. The parable says "they ALL slumbered and slept" until the midnight cry. "Then ALL those virgins arose, and trimmed their lamps." (Matt. 25:5–7) But obviously some were much too presumptuous. Their lamps needed much more than a trimming; they didn't even have oil! Please don't let it happen to you.

STRONG DELUSIONS

Both the Bible and the Spirit of Prophecy teach us that people don't become good or evil suddenly, but by a lifetime of doing right or wrong. Thus to avoid the final delusion to believe a lie will be impossible unless we have acquired a life-long habit of loving the truth, and doing right.

For instance, to snap at someone unfairly, or to mistreat anyone because we are edgy, can be a delusion to think it doesn't matter, or that it won't keep us out of heaven. If we could avoid it easily, or correct the habit, it wouldn't be a very strong delusion. But if we find it hard to correct, or think it doesn't matter, it's really dangerous. We can come to Christ just as we are, but we don't go to heaven that way, or no point in coming to Christ for help in the first place. Our goal is to love truth, not delusions. We must be like Jesus, our example. He said: "Ye have heard that it was said by them of old, Thou shalt not kill; and whosoever shall kill shall be in danger of the judgment: but I say unto you That whosoever is angry with his brother without a cause shall be in danger of the judgment." (Matt. 5:21)

So Jesus likens "anger without a cause" to killing. People don't kill people they love. And if they hate without a cause, it is a step toward murder, and Jesus takes it to its logical conclusion. You might say this is ridiculous because you wouldn't kill anybody anyways. Then why take the first step in that direction? Why not be nice, so you'll be safe to take to heaven?

But snapping at people is only one example. The same idea applies to anything else that is a deviation from the truth, or causes anyone any discomfort. Actually we are all sinners at birth. Or let's put it this way. We are all born sinners, and we have no more power to change than a leopard to change its spots. (See Jer. 13:23) This means that you and I are sinners and are powerless to change unless we love the truth as it is in Jesus and ask the Holy Spirit to help us change. This involves the very power of God to change us and has nothing to do with seminars, legislation, or will power. It doesn't take will power to eat ice cream, or to do what we love to do, even though it may tax all our might and strength. Like climbing a mountain if that's what we love to do. So we need to pray for a change of heart until we will love to do good with all our heart, and hate to do wrong with all our heart. In fact, we can't even believe that God has the power to change us except the Holy Spirit helps us to believe it. It all boils down to how we are wired up (programmed) to believe and love truth, or to believe and love error and deception. We can't redo the wiring, but God can; if we ask Him to, and obey. To obey means to start walking; to step out in faith. You walk by one step at a time. You think by tiny increments also. Then be sure you do both in the right direction.

So, does God have the power to change us, or doesn't He? It depends on what we want to believe, because God never forces the will. If we can recognize that we should change our attitude, and really want to repent, it is God which worketh in you "both to WILL and to DO of His good pleasure." (Philippians 2:13) He will give us the power to repent and change. Here is another promise of it: "If we confess our sins, he is faithful and just to forgive us our sins, and to cleanse us from all unrighteousness." (I John I: 9) Either one of these promises will make us righteous. To love God is a gift that He cannot give unless we would rather have it than sin. In our natural state we are too proud or too selfish to be made ready for heaven; to do God's will instead of our own. We want to love Jesus but keep on murdering Him. Like battered women whose husbands love them so much they beat them to death!

An axiom is a self-evident truth. For instance, two bodies cannot occupy the same space at the same time. Or, a body at rest will remain at rest unless acted upon by some outside force. Or, for every action there must be an equal and opposite reaction, etc. Likewise, in the social world, any harm or hindrance to another person is exactly opposite of love and benefit. If there seems to be no immediate reaction, it doesn't mean there isn't any. Some people may take it for a while like pressure building up inside a boiler. But sooner or later the day of reckoning must come. "Because sentence against an evil work is not executed speedily, therefore the heart of the sons of men is fully set in them to do evil." (Eccles. 8:11) The whole object of the game is for everyone to stand on their own two feet without leaning on anyone else. And unless we make a business of helping (loving) others, we lose. For "HE that is not with me is against me: and he that gathereth not with me scattereth." (Luke 11:23) We have to be completely honest to read the Bible and find out what God's will is, and let Him change us to be safe to take to heaven without contaminating the place.

MIRACLES OF THE BIBLE

"And, behold, they brought to him a man sick of the palsy, lying on a bed: and Jesus seeing their faith said unto the sick of the palsy: Son, be of good cheer; thy sins be forgiven thee. And, behold, certain of the scribes said within themselves, This man blasphemeth. And Jesus knowing their thoughts said, Wherefore think ye evil in your hearts? For whither is easier, to say, Thy sins be forgiven thee; or to say, Arise, and walk?" (Matt. 9:2-5)

There are several vital points in this story that teach us facts about miracles. One is that, to Jesus, performing a miracle was no harder than to say "Thy sins be forgiven thee; or to say, Arise, and walk." Or "What difference does it make whether I pick up a bag of potatoes with my right hand or my left, seeing I can do it either way?" Jesus had clearly cited sin as the cause of the sickness. He also proved His power and right to forgive his sins and heal him. But the scribes purposely ignored the fact that only God could work such a miracle, and thus proving that He was God in person.

Sin had somehow deranged the very molecules and chemistry of the man's body so he couldn't walk. How could He rearrange them back to normal without even touching him? We don't know, but we can think about it.

First let's consider the nuts and bolts of original creation. For instance, modern science tells us that matter is energy. The atom bomb that was exploded over Hiroshima changed less than a penny's weight of matter into energy, but it incinerated the city! Thus energy is the essence of all matter, and an atom is "the smallest unitary constituent of a chemical element, composed of a more or less complex aggregate of protons, neutrons, and electrons, whose number and arrangement determine the element."--Dictionary.

"An element (of which 102 are now recognized) cannot be separated into substances of other kinds, or at least, have hitherto resisted analysis by any known chemical means."

"An electron is an extremely small, negatively charged particle, having about one thousandth the mass of a hydrogen atom, supposed to be, or to contain the unit of negative electricity."

"A proton is a subatomic particle bearing a unitary, or electronic, positive charge of electricity, and is one of the constituents of every atomic nucleus, the number of protons in the nucleus being different for each element and called the atomic number of that element."

"A neutron is a neutral particle with approximately the same mass as a proton, but is neither positive nor negative."

"A miracle is an effect in the physical world which surpasses all known human or natural powers to accomplish or to understand, and therefore ascribed to supernatural agency." We can't understand it, but we can talk about it.

For instance, water and wine are both familiar to us. But how water, being poured into huge pots, was instantly changed into wine seems beyond our comprehension, so we call it a miracle. We know that God created all things from nothing. The wine was mostly water anyways. But even if He had had to change every single molecule from water to wine, He could do it instantly.

Now back to the sick man. Sin had rearranged the molecules in his body and made him a cripple. Jesus is God. He forgave his sin, removing the cause, then rearranged the molecules in his body to their proper place and function to restore his health.

"Sin is the transgression of the law" (I John 3:4) What law? The moral law. God's law. "For whosoever shall keep the whole law, and yet offend in one point, he is guilty of all." (James 2:10) We know the law of God to be extremely broad. So much so that except for God's mercy, all would have been lost. To infringe any part, is to infringe all, and every molecule in the man's body could have failed instantly except for God's mercy to curb it. God didn't let it go that far, but the man was crippled for life.

God's forgiveness is far different from our forgiveness. God's forgiveness is integral with His will. God's will can resurrect a body from death to life, but our will is limited by our relatively weak flesh to accomplish anything at all. "By the word of the Lord were the heavens made; and all the host of them by the breath of his mouth. For he spake, and it was done; he commanded, and it stood fast. (Ps. 33:6 and 9)

When we speak, our vocal chords move the air slightly to generate air waves we call sound, and if they understand English they get the message. When God speaks, His will is conveyed by a whole different medium than air waves, and we have no idea of the power that can create trillions of mighty suns in space! They have found one that is 90 million times bigger than our sun!

Let's say a boy gets a toy airplane for his birthday. It has a real diesel engine that fires a special fuel by compression, no spark plugs. Both the throttle and the airfoils are magnetically operated by radio control from a remote control in his hand. He stands and watches it fly wherever he directs it by radio.

All matter is energy, but all energy is not matter. Every atom is made up of electrons, protons, and neutrons whirling around each other at the speed of light. When Jesus rearranged the molecules to heal the man's palsy, He never touched the man, much less to move the atoms with a set of tongs. He may have done it by a very sophisticated remote control that could somehow change the positions and character of each molecule as they should be. All the heavenly bodies are held in orbit by gravity and momentum. A much greater power holds the atoms in orbit.

Not only can God create great suns and galaxies, but also things infinitely small. In the resurrection, He not only restores everyone's body in a moment, but also their whole lifetime of memories as well. He has a perfect record of every molecule of every person who ever lived, even to restoring their minds exactly as they were, and with perfect recall of every deed they ever committed, good or bad. Otherwise the resurrected body would be a mere blank, with no recollection of anything it ever did before, and would have no idea what it was being punished for. Even the people who died in Noah's flood. Keep this in mind next time you think God may forget, or overlook something you did. A man's soul is his body while he lives, and the exact record of it (like a blueprint) after he dies. This record is what is destroyed in hell, because God won't need it again.

THE SHAKING TIME

Earlier in these studies we discussed the status of the wise and foolish virgins, separating believers from unbelievers, the ready from the unready, etc. In every instance this means the separation of the 144000 from the rest of the church. Whenever and however it happens, it is the SHAKING TIME. It's like shaking a tree loaded with apples. The ripe ones fall off, and the unready stay right where they are. Otherwise there would be no separation, only a difference of opinion on some vital issue. All they know, or should know about last day events, will enter into their decision with eternal consequences. Most of this study is about last day events, and separating believers from unbelievers. The SHAKING is taking them down to the water, so to speak, to test them. (See Judges 7:4.)

The 144000 are all Seventh-day Adventists. God Himself is a Seventh-day Adventist. To Him the seventh day is the Sabbath, just like it is for all believers. And the Second Coming is the end of the world to Him and to us. We also believe "every word that proceedeth out of the mouth of God" to be in agreement with Him in every way, which makes us all one, and exactly what Jesus prayed for. The shaking separates those who follow Jesus, from those who merely attend church. The 144000 "loved not their lives unto the death." Death is the ultimate test. Gethsemene was the shaking time for Jesus. That was the decisive hour. The disciples all fled. They were separated at "gunpoint" so to speak. The shaking time is the decisive hour for the last true church. Also at gunpoint, as you will see from Scripture just ahead. And read Rev. 14:13 again, which comes just before the final trial. Facing the inevitable crisis (World Sunday Law) is what demands the final decision. It cannot come until the beast power demands a spurious worship. "And ALL that dwell upon the earth shall worship him, whose names are not written in the book of life of the Lamb." (Rev. 13:8) "None but those who have fortified the mind with the truths of the Bible will stand through the last great conflict." (GC 593) They must have a perfect understanding of all last day events, and know what God expects of them according to Scripture, not speculation, or tradition. Otherwise they may be only partially fortified, and Satan will certainly find their weakness. Neither can God pour out His Spirit on a defective character. He cannot trap Satan until He has the perfect 'bait' that He can depend on to see it through. God let Satan try Jesus to His death, then took Him back to heaven. When Satan killed Jesus in trying to force Him to sin, he merely sprung the trap on himself. When he does it again to the 144000 innocent followers of Jesus, he will be in the same trap all over again, and will suffer eternal hellfire for it. Thus the death of the 144000 closes probation. Then God can burn him up and cleanse the whole universe of all misunderstandings and "affliction shall not rise up the second time." (Nahum I: 9)

Early Writings has a whole chapter called "THE SHAKING." It affects the whole church at the same time. It divides God's remnant church into two parts according to their fidelity to Him, as indicated in the parable of the ten virgins. The wise virgins were READY to go in with Him to the marriage, to be His forever, thus sealing them. The foolish virgins were not prepared "to follow Him whithersoever He goeth," and to death at the World Sunday Law. They had expected to be taken to heaven "without seeing death," and not to the WAR promised in six places in Rev. 11:7, 12:17, 13:7, 13:15, 17:14, and 19:19! Please look them up. "Some will not bear this straight testimony. They will rise up against it, and this is what will cause the shaking among God's people." (EW 270) When war breaks out, they won't have to take it from the six texts above, "the straight testimony," but by then it will be too late to get ready for it, or to mend their characters with the help of the Holy Spirit, (the oil) and that door will be shut to them, according to the parable.

The Shaking Time

"There will come a time when, because of our advocacy of Bible truth, we shall be treated as traitors." (6T 394, or Last Day Events 146) Advocating Bible truth is to tell it like it is, giving the straight testimony. Having no interest in being ready leaves us without oil when the cry is made, "Behold, the Bridegroom cometh!" Please, don't let it happen to you. "Many will be imprisoned, many will flee for their lives from cities and towns, and many will be martyrs (and die) for Christ's sake in standing in defense of the truth." (3SM 397, or Last Day Events 150) But don't worry about it (not to despair anyways) because "The disciples were not endowed with the courage of the martyrs until such grace was needed." (DA 354) Then we'll have it she says. "We are not to have the courage and fortitude of martyrs of old until brought into the position they were in … .Should there be a return of persecution there would be grace given to arouse every energy of the soul to show a true heroism." (Our High Calling p.125) A bird that would fly away instantly at sight of a cat, will attack him and pick his eyes out, if he threatens her young. Same thing.

"And the dragon was wroth with the woman, and went to make war with the remnant of her seed, which keep the commandments of God, and have the testimony of Jesus Christ." (Rev. 12:17) "for the testimony of Jesus is the SPIRIT OF PROPHECY." (Rev. 19:10) Ellen White was shown "the travels of the Advent people to the Holy City"---"If they kept their eyes fixed on Jesus, who was just before them, leading them to the city, they were safe." "Soon* we heard the voice of God like many waters, which gave us the day and hour of Jesus' coming. The living saints, 144000 in number, knew and understood the voice** while the wicked thought it was thunder and an earthquake. When God spoke the time, He poured upon us the Holy Ghost, *** … .The 144000 were all sealed and perfectly united."**** (EW 15)

(*Soon) Since what she saw cannot conflict with Scripture, and since she was not given the exact time for any last day events, she could only say "soon." We have

Bible Facts About the 144,000

to go to the Bible to put everything into perspective as to time. The "time" was sealed up "until," and the word "until" is a designation of time. Ellen White could not break the time seal. "Soon" means "shortly" not a pin point of time. (See page xvii on "SOON.")

(**voice) The Bible gives us the exact time in Dan. 12:7, but only to those who hear "MY voice." "Behold, I stand at the door and knock: if any man hear MY VOICE, and open the door, I will come in to him, and will sup with him, and he with me." When? In the last days, because He is pleading to the very last generation of His church, the Laodiceans, right here. How does He knock? He offers you a chance to read and understand all last day events involving this last generation of the church, in simple language, straight from the Bible. Thus you have exactly the same advantage as any other of the 144000 believers. Does it seem reasonable that those who don't believe the Bible, when made so plain, can expect Him to force you in some way to overcome your doubt of the Scriptures? "READ" and "UNDERSTAND" are Jesus' own words in Matt.24:15 regarding the time. Time is the subject of the whole chapter of Matt.24. In Rev. 2 and 3 Jesus speaks to each of the seven churches, and to each church He says: "He that hath an ear, let him hear what the Spirit saith unto the churches," and no where except in Rev. 11:12 can we expect to hear God's voice audibly from heaven, but then we will hear in our glorified bodies, not in sinful flesh.

(***Holy Ghost) "And I will give power" is the promise at this point. (Rev. 11:3) How? "I will pour out of my Spirit upon all flesh: and your sons and your daughters shall prophesy" the exact time. (Acts 2:17) When God spoke the time, He poured out the Holy Ghost and they prophesied the time they had been given. The seal is broken the first day of the 1260 days of the beast power, which is also the little time of trouble, when God speaks the time and pours out the Holy Ghost, according to EW 85. Look it up. He comes 2595 days later. Don't take this as an audible voice from heaven. Why should He speak

114

The Shaking Time

audibly when it is written in the Bible to believers? Only those who lack faith in the Bible can be deceived to expect an audible voice. Lack of faith in the Bible leaves you under Satan's power, and he will be quick to take advantage of you.

(****united) How? By perfect obedience to 'every word that proceedeth out of the mouth of God." "They moved in exact order, like a company of soldiers." (EW 271) No human leader is mentioned; only as they follow the Bible. Any group of people who follow the same thing at the same time are automatically united. And it's not a matter of agreeing at the last minute. The 144000 are sanctified, and sanctification is the work of a lifetime. They have become new creatures in Jesus. Heavyweight champions don't suddenly become heavyweights when they enter the ring. They enter the ring because they are already heavyweights. If they weren't ready they wouldn't dare set foot in the ring. Thus the foolish virgins were shut out. They left the scene; they weren't ready, and they knew it. And when they went to get ready (went for oil) they couldn't get back in. It was too late. Can you imagine this happening to you? I hope not. That's why I try so hard to make everything so plain and simple. It has long been my personal feeling that those who are careless, and haven't tried to gain self control of their habits, and to agonize in prayer for Help, may not be led to the truth of the last days as you are reading here. Even a tiny tomato plant leans toward the light by nature. So should you. If not, how can you expect to be led of the Spirit? Let me take you through the SHAKING TIME step by step.

(EW 269)"I saw some, with strong faith and agonizing cries, pleading with God." When? During the SHAKING. And what causes the shaking? "I asked the meaning of the shaking I had seen and was shown that it would be caused by the counsel of the True Witness to the Laodiceans. (Just what you are reading right now!) This will have its effect upon the heart of the receiver, and will lead him to exalt the standard and pour forth the straight truth." About what? About last events and Bible perfection, because the shaking is close to the end of time. "Some will not bear this straight testimony. They will rise up against it, and this is what will cause a shaking among God's people."

"I saw that the testimony of the True Witness has not been half heeded. The solemn testimony upon which the destiny of the church hangs has been lightly esteemed, if not entirely disregarded. (If the whole church disregards this testimony, then the destiny of the whole church is at stake! How terrible!) This testimony must work deep repentance; all who truly receive it will obey it and be purified." Sanctified heavyweights, so to speak.

Now suddenly the next paragraph makes sense (read it) because she was having the very same vision of the 144000 that John saw at Rev. 14:2–3 where he said "and I heard the voice of harpers harping with their harps: and they sung as it were a new song before the throne, … .and no man could learn that song but the 144000."

Now Ellen White's version: "Said the angel, "List ye!" Soon I heard a voice like many musical instruments (John called them harps) all sounding in perfect strains, sweet and harmonious." Then "Said the angel, "Look ye!" My attention was then turned to the company I had seen, who were mightily shaken." John called them the 144000. "I was shown those whom I had before seen weeping and praying in agony of spirit. The company of guardian angels around them had been doubled, and they were clothed with an armor from their head to their feet. They moved in exact order, (John said they were faultless) like a company of soldiers. Their countenances expressed the severe conflict which they had endured, the agonizing struggle they had passed through. Yet their features, marked with severe internal anguish, now shone with the light and glory of heaven. They had obtained the victory, and it called forth from them the deepest gratitude and holy, sacred joy. "and no man could learn that song" What song? The song of "deepest gratitude and holy, sacred joy," she says. Singing is an expression of ecstasy. Why sing? Because they (144000) "were redeemed from

The Shaking Time

the earth" and ascended to heaven in glorified bodies. (See Rev. 11:12)

"The numbers of this company had lessened. Some (millions) had been shaken out and left by the way. The careless and indifferent, who did not join with those who prized victory and salvation enough to perseveringly plead and agonize for it, did not obtain it, and were left behind in darkness, and their places were immediately filled by others taking hold of the truth and coming into the ranks. Evil angels still pressed around them, but could have no power over them.

"I heard those clothed with the armor speak forth the truth with great power. It had effect." Upon whom? Certainly not upon their fellow church members who had been left behind in total darkness. Then who? She tells at some length in this same paragraph just who they are, and then she says "They had been hungering and thirsting for truth; it was dearer and more precious than life." So you see these are not the fellow members she spoke of near the top of the previous page who "seemed indifferent and careless," etc. So she asked, "what had made this great change. An angel answered, "It is the latter rain, the refreshing from the presence of the Lord, the loud cry of the third angel." (See EW 85) Actually, the angel who joins the third angel with an accurate message of last events from inspired Scripture.

"Great power was with these chosen ones (the 144000). Said the angel, "Look ye!" My attention was turned to the wicked, or unbelievers. (ie, the foolish virgins) They were all astir. The zeal and power with the people of God had aroused and enraged them. Confusion, confusion, was on every side. I saw measures taken against the company who had the light and power of God." What measures? The only measures the unbelieving church members could take against the 144000 would be to disfellowship them for teaching and believing other than standard doctrine set by the Church. If they (144000) don't follow the church teachings they are considered heretics. But they know they are following the Bible with the help of the Holy Spirit, and approved of God; thus the power mentioned above, which is why the ungodly are so enraged with them. Ellen White was not given a timeline for any last events. We have to go to the obvious facts in the Bible itself for the timeline here. So she doesn't even start a new paragraph for the changing scene right here. "Darkness thickened around them:" What kind of darkness? They had the victory in their personal lives, as we read above. But this is something else. "I saw them perplexed; next I heard them crying unto God earnestly. Day and night their cry ceased not: "Thy will, O God, be done! If it can glorify Thy name, make a way of escape for Thy people! Deliver us from the heathen around about us. They have appointed us unto death; but Thine arm can bring salvation. These are all the words I can bring to mind." No where in any of her writings can we find a word about the death of the 144000. Only the 144000 themselves are able to learn this song. But who are the heathen? The heathen in this case are an entirely different class from the unbelievers above. The unbelievers put them out of the church. The heathen "have appointed us unto death." And this is 3 1/2 years after they had left church. They were shaken out of the church at the beginning of the Latter Rain--Loud Cry period. They weren't put to death until they had finished their "testimony" (of Rev.14:6–11) at the end the Latter Rain, and killed at Rev.11:7. Or as Rev. 11:6 says "These have power to shut heaven, that it rain not in the days of their prophecy: and have power over waters to turn them to blood, and to smite the earth with all plagues." Their "testimony" is the three angels' messages against worshiping the beast and his image. Then the beast kills them, (closing probation) and the first plague wipes out the beast power. (See Rev. 16:2)

None of this makes sense without the timeline, "and no man could learn that song (time*) but the 144000." Why not? Because the time was sealed up "until the time of the end," until the beast is given power. Most members had foolishly neglected the oil; the prompting and enabling power of the Holy Spirit. They were not heavy-weights for God, and dared not enter the battle--the war against the beast. "Who is able to make war with him?" Rev.13:4 is the challenge. Only the Lamb of Rev.17:14, and His army is "able to make war with him." See Rev. 19:19 also. It's all one ball of wax.

(*time) Why do I say "time" here and something else somewhere else? Because a song can encompass many things; many different verses. As explained earlier, an appointment without time is no appointment; a warning without time is no warning; a prophecy without time is no prophecy. Most of this study explains the timing in last events; how to prepare for them and be ready so as not to be shaken out at the threat of war with the beast, for not knowing the time. The 144000 learn all this. And like any song, there are many different verses which they understand and sing out with all their hearts. This is the Loud Cry by the 144000 during the Latter Rain, warning the whole world not to worship the beast.

So with all we have learned so far about timing and being ready, let's read on in Early Writings 272. "All seemed to have a deep sense of their unworthiness and manifested entire submission to the will of God; yet, like Jacob, every one, without an exception, was earnestly pleading and wrestling for deliverance.

"Soon after they had commenced their earnest cry, the angels, in sympathy, desired to go to their deliverance. But a tall, commanding angel suffered them not. He said, "The will of God is not yet fulfilled. They must drink of the cup. They must be baptized with the baptism." They must die.

"Soon I heard the voice of God, which shook the heavens and the earth." Or as Rev. 11:12 says, "And they heard a great voice from heaven!!" "There was a mighty earthquake. Buildings were shaken down on every side." See the next verse 13. "I then heard a triumphant shout of victory, loud, musical, and clear. I looked upon the company, who, a short time before, were in such distress and bondage. Their captivity was turned. A glorious light shone upon them. How beautiful they then looked! All marks of care and weariness were gone, and health and beauty were seen in every countenance. Their enemies, the heathen around them, fell like dead men; they could not endure the light that shone upon the delivered, holy ones." Why not? Because in the previous paragraph above they were all killed, but she doesn't say a word about it, but Rev. 14:13 does. In this paragraph they were obviously all raised up in glorified bodies and "the heathen around them fell like dead men!" Why? Because they were now "delivered" and "holy" she says. None of this adds up unless you allow that they were all killed and returned to life in GLORIFIED BODIES. She doesn't say a word about the death of the 144000 in any of her writings. Certainly 1882 was not the time to reveal such things. Rev.11:11–12 covers both these paragraphs and their ascension to heaven. Without any timeline, Ellen White goes on to the return of Jesus, in the very next sentence, describing the general resurrection, and the glorification of the great multitude of living saints who greet Him, (I Thess. 4:13–18) all of which happens after the 1335 days of the plagues, as already explained.

So far so good. And if you are one of the 144000, and able to learn the new song, you may be able to see this same prophecy from Rev. 13 and Dan. 11. Let's try it.

When the Father sets up the beast power, it gives us the day to start counting. Speaking of the beast "And there was given unto him a mouth speaking great things and blasphemies; and power was given unto him to continue forty and two months. (1260 days). ...And it was given unto him to make war with the saints, and to overcome them: and power was given him over all kindreds, and tongues, and nations." (Rev. 13:5 and 7) "And both these kings hearts shall be to do mischief, and they shall speak lies at one table; but it shall not prosper: for yet the end shall be at the time appointed." (Dan. 11:27) Same event in both texts.

The Shaking Time

"Both kings" means the two kings of Rev. 13:7 where the beast is said "to make war with the saints, and to overcome them," and verse 15 where the other beast (of Rev. 13:11) caused "that as many as would not worship the image of the beast should be killed." Thus "their hearts shall be to do mischief" to the saints. How do we know to the saints? Because to do mischief to sinners, it would be punishment, "the wages of sin is death." Or let's put it this way, everyone else worships the beast, breaks the first commandment, and thus they deserve death; but not the saints. So to kill them is called "mischief" and not "punishment."

"But it shall not prosper." Why? Because "the ten horns (which give their power and strength unto the beast in Rev. 17:13) shall hate the whore, and shall make her desolate and naked, and shall eat her flesh, and burn her with fire." This is in verse 16, in consequence of the war. "For God hath put in their hearts to fulfill his will, and to agree, and give their kingdom unto the beast, UNTIL the words of God shall be fulfilled" vs. 17 "at the time appointed" Dan. 11:27, or at the end of the 1260 days. This power (the great whore) is judged in Rev. 18:8–24 where "her plagues come in one day, death, and mourning, and famine; and she shall be utterly burned with fire: for strong is the Lord God who judgeth her." This is only a more detailed account of Rev. 17:16, not a different event. So is Dan. 11:45, Rev. 16:2 and others which all tell of her total destruction.

But our subject is "The Shaking Time," which is brought about by the sudden confrontation of war with the beast. A war is not merely a difference of opinion. Adventists have never agreed with the beast power on religion, but it doesn't become war until somebody gets killed. And the moment it becomes a matter of life and death, the true and false are sorted out by their faith in Jesus. Some "are CALLED, and CHOSEN, and FAITHFUL" unto death in the war. (Rev. 17:14) "and they that were ready went in with him to the marriage: (to be with Him forever) and the door was shut" What door? The door of salvation. "Afterward came also the other virgins, saying, Lord, Lord, open to us. But he answered and said, Verily, I say unto you, I know you not." (Matt. 25:10–12) This is the close of probation for the church, and please don't let it happen to you. If the Holy Spirit has helped you to here, you can be helped all the way.

The Bible can't tell you everything at the same time, in the same place, so it's up to us to dig it out from various places. Four texts in Revelation mention the word WAR with the saints, and each place tells us something vital about it for our instruction. As noted earlier, each of Daniel's four visions reach to the end of the world. So it should not be surprising that the fourth should give us the exact time it is to happen. In fact, by the time it gets to Dan. 11:45 the vision has taken us through the 1260 days of the war with the saints, and to the destruction of the beast, where it says "yet he shall come to his end, and none shall help him," and the very next verse (12:1) says "and at that time thy people shall be delivered, (to heaven) every one that shall be found written in the book." Same people and same ascension as Rev. 11:12. The great time of trouble (the plagues) come at this time also.

Thus the war against the saints, that sends the beast to perdition, ends at Dan. 11:45, according to the above. And it begins at Dan. 11:27. Everything between has to apply to the 1260 days of this war against the saints. The National Sunday Law and the impending World Sunday Law is also the shaking time that closes probation for the church. The death and ascension of the 144000 brings the beast to perdition at Dan.11:45, and closes probation for the world, bringing on the plagues of Rev. 16. Earlier we found that the death of the 144000 in Rev. 11:7, 11, 12, and 15, closes probation to all. See Rev. 17:14 where the Lamb ceases to be our Intercessor. He becomes Lord of lords, and King of kings, and if need be, see also Rev. 11:6 which we studied on page 31–32, closing probation. I mention these things because they all happen with this final war between Christ and Satan at Rev. 17:14, and they are the "all these things" sworn to Daniel in answer

The Shaking Time

to his inquiry for the end of time. "And when he shall have accomplished to scatter the power of the holy people, (killed them) ALL THESE THINGS shall be finished" (Dan. 12:7) Their dead bodies are scattered all over the ground--worldwide!! If Jesus had not died for us His life would have had no POWER to save us, because He died in our stead. Likewise, the death of the 144000 perfect images of Him have the same power to witness against sin, close probation, and strengthen their converts. It springs the fatal trap on Satan, and lets God cleanse the universe of all sin forever. No second thoughts about it. All doubts are satisfied. "Affliction shall not rise up the second time." (Nahum 1:9)

In a nutshell, Daniel's vision pictures this final nightmare struggle beginning at 11:27 where the two kings "shall speak lies at one table" "to agree, and give their kingdom unto the beast" (Rev. 17:17) "to make war with the saints, and to overcome them" (Rev. 13:7) "and kill them" (Rev. 11:7) Now back to Dan.11:28 "Then shall he return into his land with great riches; (because "power was given him over all kindreds, and tongues, and nations" (Rev. 13:7) and his heart shall be against the holy covenant" (the ten commandments) "and have indignation against the holy covenant: so shall he do; he shall even return, and have intelligence (conspire) with them that forsake the holy covenant. (and betray the wise virgins) And arms shall stand on his part, and they shall pollute the sanctuary of strength, (arms means at gunpoint; sanctuary means right in church; pollute means to mess up the SDA church service!!) and shall take away the daily sacrifice, (closing probation for all church members who forsake Christ and His daily intercession) and they shall place the abomination that maketh desolate. (i.e. the Sunday Law) And such as do wickedly against the covenant (weak Adventists) shall he corrupt by flatteries: (half truths) but the people that do know their God shall be strong, (filled with the Holy Ghost, (Acts 2:17; EW85) and do exploits (miracles by the Holy Spirit) And they that understand among the people shall instruct many:

Bible Facts About the 144,000

(Acts 2:17 and Dan. 12:3) yet they shall fall by the sword, and by flame, by captivity, and by spoil, many days. Now when they shall fall, they shall be holpen with a little help: (more miracles) but many shall cleave to them with flatteries. (half lies) And some of them of understanding (the wise virgins) shall fall, to try them, and to purge, and to make them white, even to the time of the end: (of the 1260 days) because it is yet for a time appointed." (Dan.11:35)

This passage is about the war with the saints. Or as Rev. 12:17 says "And the dragon was wroth with the woman, and went to make war with the remnant of her seed, which keep the commandments of God and have the testimony of Jesus." Please notice that in Dan. 11:31, where Adventists are held at gunpoint, nobody is killed, only threatened. This only closes probation to those who forsake the faith of Jesus for fear of death at gunpoint. They are the foolish virgins who have no oil, (no H.S.) They are the ones who seek to save their lives in Luke 17:33. The Holy Ghost cannot be poured out on them because they have already denied Him. (refused to obey and perfect their faith before the day of temptation) At the time appointed, all 144000 are killed, as we saw in Rev. 11:7, which closes probation to all. We know no one is killed in Dan. 11:31, because the next verse says "but those who do know their God (the wise) shall be strong, and do exploits." They were not killed right then or they wouldn't have lived to "do exploits."

To all Adventists who think they need not know the exact timing of last day events, let me point out that those who do know the timing, and that this is only to threaten them, will not abandon Christ. But those who don't know the timing will think they are sure to be shot dead on the spot, and they give up to the enemy. They forsake Christ and the true Sabbath and accept the mark of the beast. Denying Jesus, 'the door was shut" by their own choice, because they hadn't "watched." "If therefore thou shalt not watch, I will come on thee as a thief, and thou shalt not know what hour I will come upon thee." (Rev. 3:3) and this is how He comes on the foolish virgins so unexpectedly "as a thief in the night." But if you believe the Bible timing of last day events, you will be prepared to look right down the gun barrel and know that this isn't quite the time, and won't be fooled. You will instantly be filled with the Holy Spirit (sealed) to "do exploits" and escape miraculously, just like Jesus when they tried to throw Him over the cliff. Guaranteed! Providing you call their bluff, and don't cave in to the enemy. Some do lose their lives as they "instruct many" teaching the three angels messages of Rev. 14 during the Latter Rain. "And when they shall have finished their testimony" they are killed. (Rev.11:7) You may have to reread all this over and over to really get it, and I feel sorry for our church members who have little interest in so great salvation, and in what the future holds just down the road for us.

Now we can understand Paul's explanation of His "coming" at I Thess.5:1–3. where he says, "For yourselves know perfectly (*) that the day of the Lord so cometh as a thief in the night. For when they shall say, Peace and safety: (**) then sudden destruction cometh upon them, as travail upon a woman with child; and they shall not escape."

(*) Since the "times and the seasons" were sealed up "till the time of the end" in Dan. 12:9, it was impossible for Paul's brethren in AD 54 to know the time, but absolutely essential for us to know it now that we are so near the end of time. So Paul is speaking directly to us in these last days, knowing that God would reveal the time to His very elect at just the right time for them to know it "perfectly."

(**) Apparently Paul had been shown this whole sad story of Dan. 11:31, testing the entire SDA Church at gunpoint at midnight. The World Sunday Law is to follow The National Sunday Law, so it will have been brewing for some time, to become legal at midnight. No doubt every Adventist will be in their churches praying for deliverance. Since they keep all ten commandments, and all

27 doctrines of the church, and are all in church praying to God, confidently saying "Peace and safety," and expecting Him to protect them, they can't imagine sudden destruction. But only the very elect have learned "without exception" how to "agonize in prayer" when they need Help. And only the very elect (144000) are faultless before the throne of God, and have reached Bible perfection. "They loved not their lives" and are only too happy to lay down their lives at any moment for Jesus. Certainly they wouldn't deny Him at this point, for to them their death means the "marriage" to be His forever, and "sealed." But to the rest of the church, because they have never known Him, (trusted Him) they deny Him and surrender to the police as Sunday keepers, to save their lives temporarily, erroneously expecting to be translated, "without tasting death." But Jesus says "I know you not." (Matt. 25:12) Now you see why I couldn't explain these things before.

Before we leave this chapter on the "Shaking time" we need to understand one other thing. Of necessity our church denomination is forced to maintain church standards in order to prevent serious differences of opinion, quarreling over doctrines, schisms, etc. Please do not think that anything in these studies is meant to cause serious misunderstandings in the church before the time of God's own sealing of His servants. We are to be wise as serpents, and harmless as doves. We are not to debate the facts of last day events in church, which we are strictly warned against doing. We are only to know and understand them ourselves, and to teach secretly (clothed in sackcloth) those who love truth, and are watching. Ellen White warned: "You will take passages in the "Testimonies" that speak of the close of probation, of the shaking among God's people, and you will talk of a coming out from this people of a purer, holier people that will arise. (Exactly what you are reading here based on Scripture) Now all this pleases the enemy … .Should many accept the views you advance, and talk and act upon them, we would see one of the greatest fanatical excitements that has ever been witnessed among Seventh-day Adventists.

The Shaking Time

This is what Satan wants." (ISM 179) (1890). This is exactly what I have done in compiling this study, except for one important difference. And what is that? Time! Over a century has gone by since 1890, and now we are near the harvest of the world. Can you imagine a farmer being led somehow to start harvesting, mowing down a crop in mid season, (1890) long before it was mature. But Satan would be equally delighted to have us completely ignore all preparation for the harvest time now that it is right upon us. Satan is the enemy, and he knows that mistiming can be fatal, especially if he can fool us by a century or more. Besides, in 1882 Ellen White herself wrote "The Shaking" in Early Writings (269–272) of this very same separation, saying, "Confusion, confusion, was on every side," etc. In 1890 she was speaking about 1890, but in EW she was definitely speaking to us, (in vision) so near the end of time. Misplaced prophecy is Satan's attempt to destroy and contradict God as he always does if he can. Thus we are warned to "watch" and to know the difference.

If last day events are not to be taught openly in church, then how are the wise and foolish virgins of the church to be separated? Answer. At gunpoint as we just read in Dan. 11:31–35! If the Bible and 50 some odd SOP books don't have enough power to sort us out, certainly no living man, or men, will be able to judge our hearts and issue each one a visa to enter heaven! But at gunpoint, each saint will decide for himself whether he has been true to the Holy Spirit, or if he is a fake. Every saint is a willing and cheerful volunteer in Christ's army in the war against the beast, as pointed out clearly above, and I'm sorry to be so blunt, or heartless, or graphic, as if you have no feelings. I would gladly do anything to temper the facts, if I could, but if you are to be among the 144000 you will be able to "learn that song" just as it is in the Bible. If I try to change it to something different it wouldn't be "that song" any more. It would be Bernie's song; my version of it to save hurting your feelings. But if you were to follow some distorted version of it you would be lost for not taking the Bible as it reads. God puts all this information into your hands; don't thank me for it, and I certainly couldn't have done it without the aid of the Holy Spirit. I can't teach these things in church. Neither can I circulate this script openly or indiscriminately (casting pearls before swine) or give it to careless church members that I know are not living up to all the light they have. If they are already rejecting light, they will have no relish for any more, and will turn on me personally, as they have.

I didn't write these things to help you anyways. I wrote them merely to satisfy my own interest in Bible study, and nobody else was even slightly interested in what I was doing. Nobody wanted to read it, nor hear it. Thus I was completely free of anyone else's influence, or risk of leading anyone astray. I could try anything on paper, and I did; not worrying about how crazy it sounded. Without any ulterior motive, I had no reason to twist or warp anything, but to follow exactly what the Word said, step by step, no matter how it sounded. Only after thirty years, and seeing a tiny ad in a magazine, I finally thought of rewriting the whole thing adaptable to help others in a book. During those same long years the world had changed dramatically, and I began to realize the Holy Spirit had been helping me step by step without even suspecting why it had all come together so well.

SO WHAT DO WE DO NOW?

Providing we have a correct understanding of things to this point, and if we want to be among the 144000, we ought to act accordingly. And how is that? Well, if I expected to be a doctor, I think I ought to begin to study medicine right away. Why wait until somebody needs a heart transplant and expect God to enable me to do it without any preparation for it? How would you like to have me operate on you? Repent and get right with God right away. Millionaires think like millionaires in order to be one. The 144000 will all have the mind of Christ, and reflect His image. As a man thinketh, so is he.

Doctors and ministers feel CALLED to their vocation. They study diligently for years, and if they don't faint, they graduate. Then they intern to practice what they have learned. Finally they are CHOSEN, or hired to some field of endeavor. If they are FAITHFUL they actually save lives, either in this world, or the next. Thus they are called, chosen, and faithful to the purpose of their calling.

Now let's see how this applies to the 144000. "These (Satan's army) shall make WAR with the Lamb, and the Lamb shall overcome them: for he is Lord of lords, and King of kings: and they that are with him are CALLED, and CHOSEN, and FAITHFUL." (Rev. 17:14)

When were they CALLED? When they heard "the still small voice" of truth, and were baptized in the name of the Father, the Son, and the Holy Ghost, thus having their names written in "the book of life of the Lamb."

When were they CHOSEN? When they volunteered to enter the ring as heavyweights, so to speak, in the war against the beast.

Bible Facts About the 144,000

When were they FAITHFUL? When they "loved not their lives unto the death" following the Lamb "whithersoever he goeth," in the war.

Everyone who is baptized into the church, renouncing the world, is CALLED to be perfect, "even as your Father in heaven is perfect." (Matt. 5:48) But unfortunately, very few take it that seriously. They sit in church for fifty years, dying of old age, never seeming to catch the vision of Bible perfection, or making any reasonable progress in that direction. Sitting in church for fifty years may make you one of 16 million members, but not one of the 144000 who are forgiven and have clean, "holy hearts" as Ellen White says on p. 32 of 2SM.

Since 1844 God has been waiting for 144000 to reach perfection; to be master surgeons, so to speak, just like their perfect Example; even raising the dead, if need be. We all have the same Book. We all know how to read. But somehow we seem to miss the whole object of the Book, which is completely self explanatory if we would only believe it.

Let's say April 15 is the day of reckoning; the judgment day. Knowing how to add and subtract doesn't determine my income tax, but it helps. It can't be done until after December 31, but if I neglect to do it by April 15 I'm already wicked by default. I can't be ready if I completely disregard the time. Dear IRS: Please cancel my subscription to your 1040, etc. "The Lord of that servant shall come in a day when he looketh not for him, and in an hour he is not aware of, and shall cut him asunder, and appoint him his portion with the hypocrites: there shall be weeping and gnashing of teeth" (Matt. 24:50–51) coming on us "as a thief in the night".

I do not pretend to know all we will need to know about all these things, nor that I have made no mistakes in the work to here. I have tried to obey as honestly as I know how, in searching the Bible for last day events, and to present them as palatable as the case allows without distortion. If you have a better explanation about it, please let's study it

So What Do We Do Now?

some more together. In many places I have explained things differently than others before me. Please do not think my work excludes all previous works which have served God's purposes to now. Prove all things and judge honestly.

WHY GOD RISKED EVERYTHING FOR US

"And shouldest destroy them which destroy the earth." (Rev.11:18) Everyone knows that man has created a weapon that is capable of making the whole earth uninhabitable. We know the circumstances that brought us to the atom bomb. We were afraid Hitler might beat us to it. Once we had it, we couldn't keep it out of enemy hands, and now the rogue nations have it to threaten one another until trouble threatens disaster! This is what the power of imagination can do in the hands of the wicked, for without the power of imagination there could be no atom bomb nor any kind of creative effort; no music, no poetry, no invention, no progress of any kind. Not even worship, for which God risked all to give us the power of imagination. In order to be able to worship Him, He gave us this power, which is basically the power of choice. This is the subject of this chapter.

It goes like this. As a general rule, the more a thing is meant for good, the more evil it can cause if misused, or misapplied, by the power of imagination. Love can turn to hate, and hate to war. Sex was meant to populate the earth, but adultery (misuse) reeks havoc. Computers can speed up business, or spread crime and corruption ad infinitum. And all of the above depend on the power of imagination. So is imagination the problem? No. The problem is self control. "Come now, and let us reason together, saith the Lord: though your sins be as scarlet, they shall be as white as snow; ... . If ye be willing and obedient, (self control) ye shall eat of the good of the land; but if ye refuse and rebel, (no self control) ye shall be devoured with the sword;" (Isaiah 1:18–20)

So God gave us imagination, a very dangerous and all powerful weapon, making us somewhat equal to Himself,

Why God Risked Everything for us

and to make worship possible, for His own pleasure, and for ours. But if He then put up a wall between Him and us, or if He limited the range of this weapon toward Himself, we would automatically assume that He didn't really trust us with it. He would be the cause of doubt, not trust and love, and could be blamed for opening the door to sin.

Let's say a man falls in love, and marries his sweat heart, but then she notices him checking his food for poison! She sees that he doesn't trust her after all, and thinks he must have had a change of heart. Trust begets trust, and doubt begets doubt. "We love Him, because He first loved us." (I John 4:19) "There is no fear (doubt) in love; but perfect love casteth out fear: because fear hath torment. He that feareth (doubts) is not made perfect in love." (Verse 18.) Love and fear (doubt) are contrary one to the other. To entertain one is to deny the other.

So God ran the risk. Only perfect love and trust satisfies the heart. Anything less is abject misery. If any doubt should arise, He would rather lose His life than to use any cowardly safeguards to prevent it. No protective wall between. It was a matter of all or nothing. Doubt (sin) did arise and God died in order to put away all doubt forever. Christ (God) was taken by force and murdered as a common criminal. He was taken by force, but only because He offered no resistance whatever. No wall between. He didn't use His divinity as a wall to protect Himself from the crucifixion.

"As soon then as He said unto them, 'I am He,' they went backward, and fell to the ground." (John 18:6) They were instantly and completely overwhelmed, and the same power could certainly have kept them in check indefinitely, which they understood perfectly. Yet His object was not to save Himself, but to release His disciples, which He bargained for as soon as He let them up. He also gave them another proof that He was their Master as He miraculously restored the ear of one of His enemies.

Crucifixion is a long, lingering death. Life ebbs away slowly and ends in a coma. In a coma He would have been unconscious, and not able to "cry again with a loud voice, yielding up the ghost." So He gave His life of His own free will, and while very much alive.

We take it for granted that since He predicted His own resurrection, He knew He would be dead only a few hours. We tend to forget that Jesus was a prophet. A prophet speaks under inspiration. That means He is moved by the Spirit of God, and "not by the will of man." A prophet seldom comprehends the words he speaks. We read earlier where Ellen White's mind was locked from understanding the Scriptures for two or three years. (See page 42.) And when Isaac asked Abraham about the lamb for the sacrifice, he said (not even realizing that he was speaking under inspiration) "My son, God will provide Himself a lamb for a burnt offering." (Gen. 22:8) But when Abraham raised the knife to slay his only son, he knew nothing of the lamb caught in the thicket until God revealed it to him. The words he had told Isaac had never registered in his mind.

Likewise, nothing was plainer to Christ than that if He died in man's stead, it was impossible to save both Himself and man. Consequently He cried, "My God, My God, why hast thou forsaken me?" because He felt exactly the same hopeless despair that every sinner must feel who dies without hope. And if Christ had not died in the same hopeless despair as any common sinner, with no hope whatever, He was a fake, and never tasted the second death for me at all. I believe that, just as surely as God locked Ellen White's mind from comprehending Scripture for two or three years, He also forsook Jesus on the cross. Jesus would have been lying in saying God had forsaken Him, if He had died with any idea He would be resurrected a few hours later, and who would dare say He was acting out a lie? Not me!

You and I can die with the full assurance of the resurrection by faith in Christ, providing we have let Him cleanse us of all unrighteousness. But if He had died with the full assurance that it was only for a few hours, how much love would that have inspired in us to love Him in return? And besides, it could not have meant dying forever in order to pay our penalty. Jesus is no fake, and the better we understand His completely honest sacrifice for us, the more we are bound to love Him for it. No wonder John said there wasn't room enough in the whole world to contain the books to tell about His love for us.

EXAGGERATING JESUS

We've probably all heard about the little boy bragging about how strong his father is. People who brag a lot have a tendency to stretch things a little, but there is no danger of doing that about Jesus, because it is impossible to exaggerate anything about Him. For instance, can you exaggerate His power? He told His disciples; "All power is given unto me in heaven and in earth." (Matt. 28:18) This means that if there was any kind of power He lacked, He couldn't say He had it ALL. So we certainly can't exaggerate His power.

Modern astronomy claims there are about 200 billion stars in our Milky Way Galaxy, which is only an average sized galaxy. With the Hubble telescope they estimate there are about 200 billion galaxies out there. There is talk of building a telescope ten times the power of the Hubble, and even that may not see the edge of the universe! Yet the Bible says, "All things were made by Him; (Jesus) and without Him was not anything made that was made." (Heb. 1:3)

To get a little idea how much energy this represents, the bomb that was dropped on Hiroshima changed nearly a penny's weight of matter into energy, but it incinerated the city. Our sun changes about 4 million tons of matter into energy every second, and it is only an average sized star. They have found a star 90 million times as big as our sun. Also one that weighs 50 times our planet that is moving at 2 million miles an hour. Jesus made it, heated it up white hot and started it up to that speed!

The Hubble can detect light from 14 billion light years away; in all four directions, which means lot of area. So Jesus is very strong.

Exaggerating Jesus

Now back to our subject. Can we exaggerate His age? No we can't because the Bible says He has "neither beginning of days, nor end of life" (Heb. 7:3) He always was, and always will be.

Can we exaggerate His intelligence? Not a bit. Col. 2:3 says that in Christ are hid all the treasures of wisdom and knowledge. He knows the end from the beginning, and He knows everything.

Some people spend their lives trying to master the game of chess. Others the violin, or the piano, or mathematics, or astronomy, etc. ad infinitum. But no human can master everything. Sooner or later some little kid comes along to beat them flat out.

Can we exaggerate the love of Jesus? John 3;16 says "For God so loved the world that he gave His only begotten son, that whosoever believeth in him should not perish, but have everlasting life." The world's greatest preachers have worn themselves out preaching on the love of Jesus, and haven't told the half of it.

On Moody's first trip to England in 1867 he met Henry Moorhouse, the boy preacher. Moorhouse was a beardless boy of 17 who wanted to come to America and preach for Moody. Moody tried to put him off several times, because he didn't look as if he could preach at all. He didn't even have a big bushy beard like Moody. Who would ever listen to him?

But finally Moorhouse showed up in Chicago wanting to preach. Moody had to be out of town a few days and asked the officers of the church to give him a try on Thursday night. Friday night would be the regular prayer meeting, and after hearing him they could decide whether to let him speak again, or just have their regular meeting. Moody said he would be back Saturday and if he spoke well maybe he could take Moody's place at the Sunday meetings and he would just listen.

So when Moody got back on Saturday he asked his wife how the young Englishman was coming along and if the people liked him.

"They like him very much," she said.

"Did you hear him?"

"Yes, I did."

"Well, did you like him?"

"Yes, I like him very much. He preached two sermons on John 3:16 and I think you will like him, although he preached a little differently from you."

"How is that?"

"Well, he tells the worst enemies that God loves them."

"Then he's wrong." Moody replied.

"But I think you will agree with him when you hear him, because he backs up everything he says with the Bible."

Sunday morning Moody noticed that everyone had brought their Bibles and Moorhouse preached. He gave chapter and verse for every statement he made, and Moody said he had never heard anything like it.

Sunday night the church was packed and Moorhouse preached John 3:16 again, the most extraordinary sermon Moody had ever heard. He didn't divide the text into "secondly" and "thirdly" and "fourthly," he just took the whole verse and went through the whole Bible from Genesis to Revelation to prove that in all ages God loved the world. God sent patriarchs and prophets and holy men to teach us, then He sent His own Son, and after they killed Him, He sent the Holy Ghost. Moody said he knew God loved us, but not that much, and he just couldn't keep back the tears.

It's pretty hard to get people to church on Monday nights, but they came to hear Moorhouse, and they brought their Bibles. Again he preached on John 3:16

and showed along a whole different line from Genesis to Revelation that God loves us. He could turn to any part of the Bible and prove it, and this was the best one yet.

Tuesday night came and he still preached John 3:16, but on an even higher plain, because he was getting a better foundation to build on. For seven nights straight he preached John 3:16 and each one better than before. Moorhouse taught Moody to draw the sword full length, to fling away the scabbard, and battle with the naked blade. So, you cannot exaggerate the love of God in Jesus.

As Moorhouse finished on the seventh night he said, "If I could borrow Jacob's ladder and climb up into heaven, and ask Gabriel to tell how much God loves the world, all he could say would be: "God so loved the world that he gave his only begotten Son, that whosoever believeth in him should not perish, but have eternal life." (From "A Biography of D. L. Moody by his Son" p. 137–143.)

Let's say a man becomes a billionaire by his own honest talent, and he wants a wife to share it with. Do you think he would be interested in a second hand wife? Do you think he would accept a tiny flaw in a wife? Neither will God. Especially when He has the power to cleanse her from all unrighteousness if she be willing in order to be His forever. (See I John I: 9) "Let us be glad and rejoice, and give honor to him: for the marriage of the Lamb is come, and his wife hath made herself ready. And to her was granted (given freely) that she should be arrayed in fine linen, clean and white; for the fine linen is the righteousness of saints." (Rev. 19:7–8)

If you look up the word "white" in Strong's you will see that it means radiant. Snow is clean and white, but not radiant. Snow makes no light of its own on a dark night, but if it were radiant, it would be as light as the noonday sun. And not merely ordinary light, but like the angel that rolled away the stone from Christ's tomb. "His countenance was like lightning, and his raiment white as snow: And for fear of him the keepers did shake and became as dead men." (Matt. 28:3–4) This should help us to understand Daniel 12:3: "And they that be wise shall shine as the brightness of the firmament; and they that turn many to righteousness as the stars for ever and ever." This is the robe of light mentioned in the Forward.

Let's just mention a few safe rules and guidelines for help. Be quick to repent as soon as you discover an error in your life or thinking, as Peter did at the foot washing in John 13. Be faithful in prayer and worship as Daniel was in the lion's den. (Daniel 6) "Pray without ceasing." (2 Thess. 5:17) "Check everything by the Bible as "those in Thessalonica, in that they received the word with all readiness of mind, and searched the scriptures daily, whether those things were so." (Acts 17:11) Whenever in doubt, ask yourself, "What would Jesus do?"

HOW GOD MADE THE SABBATH

"By the word of the Lord were the heavens made; and all the host of them by the breath of his mouth." "For he spake, and it was done; he commanded, and it stood fast." (Psalms 33:6 and 9) And Gen. 1:16 says, "And God made two great lights; the greater light to rule the day, and the lesser light to rule the night; he made the stars also." So when did He make the stars? On the fourth day. (See verse 19) The fourth day is Wednesday; so He made all the stars on Wednesday afternoon just before quitting time.

Modern astronomers claim there are about 200 billion stars in our Milky Way Galaxy. Also with the Hubble Space Telescope they say there are about 200 billion galaxies out there. So if He could make 200 billion galaxies on an afternoon, why did it take Him seven days to create our little world? Simple! The Bible says God cannot lie. (See Titus 1:2) and not even God can create a seventh day Sabbath in less than seven days without lying about it! So the 7th day Sabbath took Him longer than all else put together, and thus the most important, because it's His memorial (flag) of His kingdom.

We know that this world was created only 6000 years ago, including the 200 billion galaxies, which the Hubble proves to reach out about 14 billion light years away! Can we explain this 14 billion light years versus 6000 years from the Bible? Why not?

Adam and Eve were created as fully mature human beings; not babies. "And God made great whales;" not baby whales. (Vs. 21) The trees were also created fully mature, and bearing fruit so Adam didn't have to wait months or years for a lunch. The trees no doubt also could have had their full quota of annular rings in their trunk wood. Certainly if God could make apple wood, and peach, and oak, and maple, He could also create annular rings in them the very first day. This is only a difference of texture, not substance. Not that it would matter anyways. And if He could fill the sky with mighty galaxies, He shouldn't have had too much trouble making them fully mature with 14 billion years of light between them. All matter is energy going in circles at the speed of light. So the stars are made of energy going in circles. Light is power going in straight lines. As a rule, straight lines are easier to make than circles. So let's not assume that He couldn't stretch light out in lines 14 billion years long on Wednesday afternoon. Only an evolutionist would balk at common sense logic like this.

We have seen that the final controversy will be a contest between Sabbath and Sunday keeping. Sin entered this world when Adam and Eve stole the forbidden fruit. For thousands of years mankind has been stealing God's holy day, the seventh day, which He reserved for all creation to remember Him by forever. "Wherefore the children of Israel shall keep the Sabbath, to observe the Sabbath throughout their generations, for a perpetual covenant. It is a sign between me and the children of Israel for ever; for in six days the Lord made heaven and earth, and on the seventh day he rested, and was refreshed." (Ex. 31: 16–17) Many people pay little or no attention to their national flag during peace time, but will die for it if their country is threatened. Likewise the Seventh day Sabbath is like a flag between God's people and Satan's. Same thing. No wonder God made it a memorial of His whole creation, and the most important of all the ten commandments! To threaten your flag is to threaten everything, and true believers will die for their flag; the seventh day Sabbath.

We walk by putting one foot ahead of the other. We think from one idea to another, from fact to fact, line upon line, here a little and there a little. Do not reject a known truth. If it doesn't fit right away, it may latter. Write it down where you can find it. Edison kept good records of his experiments. Ellen White kept diaries and notes of everything she knew and did. Keep your eyes open, and your mind sharp. Don't waste time on trifles. Read the classics and the Bible. Use the dictionary, and the concordance even for the minutiae. Be mentally honest scrupulously. Don't interrupt a train of thought, or a brain storm; it may never come back to you again. The more you practice all these things, the sooner God will need you desperately for the glory of His name and work.

If anyone reading this thinks I might be one of the 144000, let me explain something. "The experience of the new birth does not destroy the old nature. It is brought into subjection and is placed under control of the Spirit, but it is not eradicated. To the truthfulness of this fact every Christian can testify. Immediately to destroy all evil propensities would be to remove the new convert from all possibility of temptation. There could be no testing and trying, no growing in grace, no trusting in the keeping power of Christ to prevent from falling, no further mortifying of the flesh, and no watching unto prayer. The surrender of the soul to the control of the Spirit is tantamount to a declaration of war between the Spirit and the flesh. Hitherto the flesh has had full sway, and the general tendency has been downward. Now the flesh has been placed in a state of "crucifixion," but not of actual death. The flesh pleads for recognition; stirred up by Satan, it seeks to regain the ascendency of power. "For the flesh lusteh against the Spirit, and the Spirit against the flesh: and these are contrary the one to the other." (Gal. 5:17) There is, therefore, no co-operation of the flesh with the Spirit in the new creation. Paul understood this when he declared: "I delight in the law of God after the inward man: but I see another law in my members, warring against the law of my mind, and bringing me into captivity to the law which is in my members." (Romans 7:21–23)" ("The Holy Spirit" by W. H. Branson p. 67.)

So I'm not a bit better off than you are in being one of the 144000. Writing this book in no way excuses me from "crucifying" my flesh totally, but it did help fix things clearly in my mind. I am fully aware of the problems of temptation, which are basically covetousness and pride. Read EW266–269 and let it sink in. I have tried several times to read "Fox's Book of Martyrs," but it was too gruesome. It finally occurred to me that the Holy Spirit had strengthened them by filling their hearts with the love of Jesus. Thus the love of Jesus had to be stronger than the pain, or it couldn't have enabled them as it did, and that says it all. So they were able to surrender fully, and gladly suffered such cruelty, singing hymns as their arms dropped off in the fires at the stake. "The disciples were not endowed with the courage and fortitude of the martyrs until such grace was needed." (DA 354, Last Day Events 150) This will help us with any other temptations, or crisis in our lives, if we hold Him to His promise as Jacob did.

Every saint of the 144000, without exception, must agonize in prayer in the shaking time, which is still ahead. "EVERY ONE, without an exception, was earnestly pleading and wrestling for deliverance." (EW 272) This is a must to be among the 144000. If you don't know how to agonize in prayer you may have never become very alarmed about a serious besetment in your life, but you must in order to be like Jesus. Paul said, "I am exceeding joyful in all our tribulation." (2 Cor. 7:4) Was he a glutton for misery? No, but without tribulation there could be no "crucifying" of the flesh, nor chance to build up spiritual muscle and strength to stand in the time of trouble.

Anyhow, please don't discount my book just because it was written by one who has sinned like everyone else. At this point I think my future looks pretty bright, and I hope I have brightened yours also. Einstein said he didn't have any special talent, but he had "extreme curiosity." Likewise God's saints may not be so talented, but desperately hungry for HIS righteousness.

To resist or reject a known truth is to sin against the Holy Spirit and commit the unpardonable sin. It shuts the door, and we no longer hear Him knock, thus it closes probation in our case. (See p. 46)

How God Made the Sabbath

God will not give us more light until we use the light we have, which effectively closes probation to us also. (See p. 48–51)

Our baptism declares "war between the Spirit and the flesh" which we must surrender to be "crucified" totally. (see p. 143)

"And I, if I be lifted up from the earth, will draw all men unto me." (John 12:32) How does He draw us? By His love. It's a gift. To refuse this gift is the unpardonable sin. To love anything is a pleasure. I love to play my violin. To me it's a pleasure, not work, to improve my playing. Also I love to be like Jesus, and it's a pleasure, not work, to become like Him more and more. To study music helps my playing. To study the Bible helps me love Jesus, and to want to please Him more. I have a very visible muscle on the side of my left hand from many years of straining to reach high notes on my violin, but not on my right hand. For many years, especially since working on last day events, I have made real progress in my spiritual life from a much closer attention to Jesus and the Holy Spirit. Recently I completed a span of seven full weeks without a single known sin of any kind that I was aware of. It has been over forty years since I have had to apologize to anyone at a foot washing service. It was so humiliating that I have avoided offence at any cost, not to have to make amends that way again. "He that gathereth not with me scattereth abroad." (Matt. 12:30) We must be gaining spiritually, and be free of all offence consistently in our lives before probation closes. It closes the first day of the 1260 days of the Latter Rain, for which there is no count-down period to know.

"Now when Jesus was risen early the first day of the week, he appeared first to Mary Magdalene, out of whom he had cast seven devils." (Mark 16:9) But she had to be willing to be free of them, because He never forces the will. And in Mark 5 He cast out a legion of devils from one man. I have no idea how many I had, but I must have had plenty, as I suppose everyone has. The 144000 must be free of all devils for some indefinite period before we can be filled with the Holy Spirit on the first day of the 1260 day Latter rain, and there is no count-down for that day. We have to be ready for it. Our characters cannot be changed at the last minute like a deathbed experience, but we have plenty of time before hand, unless we refuse to respond to the Saviour's love that draws us.

Satan hates me and I've had my share of troubles. During the years of working on this script my house has been on fire seven times! Within a mile and a half of my house, a huge sawmill and six houses have burned flat, and three others completely gutted! I fell on the ice and tore the cords completely off my right shoulder, and partially off the other one twelve years later. One day I drove 270 miles, and got home safely, but the very next day I backed 20 feet out of my driveway and the tie rod fell off! I still have it with the threads completely worn out! My wife had cancer in both lungs for six years, and went to the hospital 14 times by ambulance. She finally had a stroke in January, pneumonia in March, and died April 8, 2006. By July 2007 we would have celebrated our sixtieth anniversary. We had two boys, but one was born mentally handicapped.

"He sat by a furnace of sevenfold heat as he watched by the precious ore, And closer he bent with a searching gaze as he heated it more and more. So he waited there with a watchful eye, with a love that is strong and sure; And His gold didn't suffer a whit more heat than was needed to make it pure."---Selected

Again let me quote Philippians 2:12–14 "Work out your own salvation with fear and trembling. For it is God which worketh in you both to will and to do of his good pleasure. Do all things without murmurings and disputings." In other words, we mustn't drag our feet or complain about how God disciplines us. He only does what He has to for our sake, and not for the fun of it. There is no way this book can say what that is in your case, but if it has caused you to do something about it, it will have served its purpose. There isn't much time, so we all have to agonize in prayer for help to see and to forsake every sin, and to be faultless before the throne. We are in the sealing time, which is very, very short, and it will soon be too late to correct anything at all. God bless.

We'd love to have you download our catalog of
titles we publish at:

www.TEACHServices.com

or write or email us your thoughts,
reactions, or criticism about this
or any other book we publish at:

TEACH Services, Inc.
254 Donovan Road
Brushton, NY 12916

info@TEACHServices.com

or you may call us at:

518/358-3494